"History is a cruel trick played on the dead by the living."
—Old Vaquero saying

"In the darkness, Death crouched, waiting, ready."
—Walter Noble Burns

Imagine
finding an old trunk full of
all the missing pictures!

First Edition

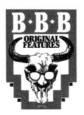

BOOK ONE

EL CHIVATO
THE INFANT RASCAL

AN ILLUSTRATED HISTORY

BY BOB BOZE BELL
A LIMITED EDITION

February 8, 1517
Francisco de Córdoba is the first white man to touch the mainland of Mexico. He is blown there while trying to get from Cuba to the Bahamas in quest of Indian slaves.

1598, Juan De Oñate leads an expedition into New Mexico via the Camino Real (Royal Road). Only 275 years until He comes.

September 16, 1810
Father Hidalgo rings a bell. He rings it in the morning. He rings it in the evening. He rings it all over this land. It's the bell of freedom. It's the bell of justice.

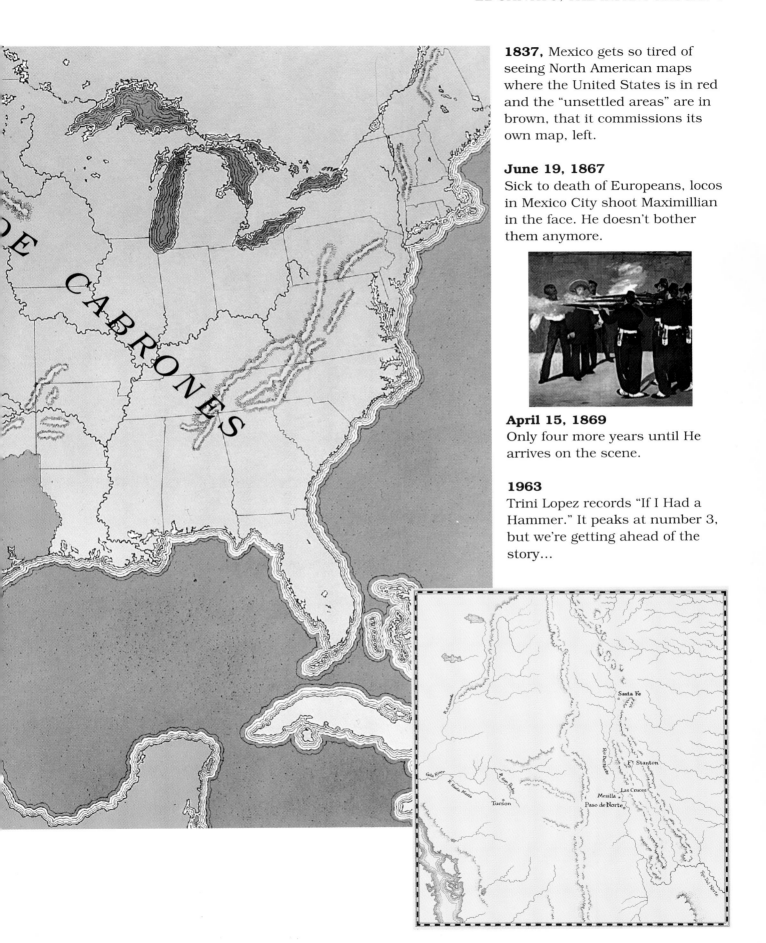

1837, Mexico gets so tired of seeing North American maps where the United States is in red and the "unsettled areas" are in brown, that it commissions its own map, left.

June 19, 1867
Sick to death of Europeans, locos in Mexico City shoot Maximillian in the face. He doesn't bother them anymore.

April 15, 1869
Only four more years until He arrives on the scene.

1963
Trini Lopez records "If I Had a Hammer." It peaks at number 3, but we're getting ahead of the story…

Fort Sumner, 1868

After several years in captivity at Fort Sumner, New Mexico territory, 8,000 Navajos are "allowed" to walk home. As the Dineh ("The People" in Navajo) trek westward towards the four sacred mountains, an old Holy Man is asked where they are coming from. He replies,

——— **"Muerte."**

Summer, 1868

John Chisum lays claim to most of the land south of Fort Sumner. He has no legal title, but insists on "the right of discovery." It sticks.

The Board of Officers Recommendations

Anglo officers meet at Fort Sumner, April 26, 1865 to hammer out a form of government for the Navajos – "these Indians have got to be made to respect the bonds which unite civilized society." Example:

ARTICLE 6. *Any adult Indian who shall be found absent from his or her village between the hours of 7 o'clock p.m. and 5 o'clock a.m. in winter, and 8 o'clock p.m. and 4 o'clock a.m. in summer, shall be imprisoned as in article 3.*

The Recommendations are recorded by **Lawrence G. Murphy,** Captain 1st Cav. New Mexico Volunteers.

**(left) Henry McCarty, age 4
(below) Young Henry plays with his father as his mother looks on. Taken about 1865, the location is unknown.**

February 11, 1873

A wagon loaded with earthly possessions and hope heads south from Denver, Colorado. In it are Mr. William H. Antrim, Catherine McCarty and her two sons – Josie and Henry (later to become Billy).

Catherine is sick with "incipient consumption" (tuberculosis). And now they are heading out of the United States to a place where she can "equalize the circulation of the blood" and breathe "the purest atmosphere in the grandest country that no pen can describe!" Or at least that's what the handbill they picked up in Denver promises.

Saturday, March 1, 1873

Mr. William H. Antrim and Mrs. Catherine McCarty, both of Santa Fe, New Mexico are joined in matrimony by the Reverend David F. McFarland of the First Presbyterian Church. The witnesses are Harvey Edmonds, Mrs. A.R. McFarland, her daughter Katie, and Mrs. McCarty's two sons, Josie and Henry.

February, 1873

Just north of Fort Union on the Old Santa Fe Trail, Henry and his older brother, Josie, witness their first Mexican *vaqueros*. The two boys stand atop the tailgate and watch in awe as the *charros* sweep by.

Bold and graceful, the three Spanish cowboys look like land-locked, prairie pirates to the wide-eyed boys. Shouting in their strange tongue, the three horse-men thunder through the wet grass, their lean ponies kicking up clods of black earth as their silver, studded saddles glisten in the clear, New Mexican light.

Spring, 1873

Mescalaro Apaches raid Chisum's Bosque Grande Ranch in the middle of the night, steal-ing every horse on the premises (125). None of the dogs bark. Even though the Apaches are operating on the "right of discov-ery" principle, Uncle John is not amused.

March 12, 1873

From Santa Fe, the Antrim family catches the trail down the Rio Grande, headed for Silver City.

Progress is slow but the American family is learning Spanish "a mile a minute."

One of the first words young Henry learns is "cabrón," which is an insult – loosely translated it means "bastard."

When they happen onto a funeral procession west of Isleta, Henry and Josie learn the word for death – "muerte."

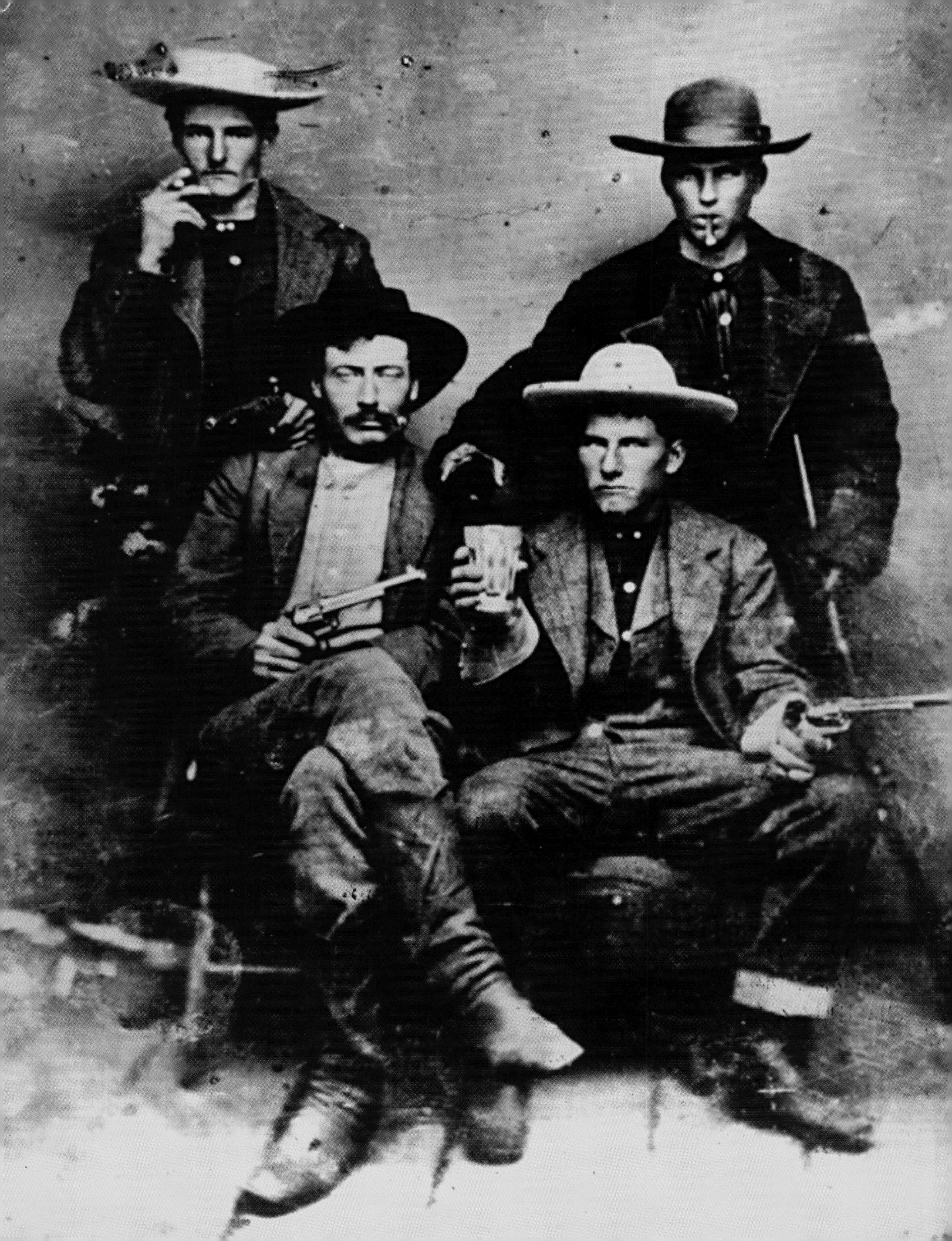

Rough fellows in a row

"...a wild breed, born to the saddle on the Texas plains, as skillful horsemen as the world ever knew, as adept in gun play as in horsemanship, rough fellows in a row; courage and loyalty as much a part of their heritage as hardship and danger."

– WALTER NOBLE BURNS

John Chisum, Cattle king of New Mexico

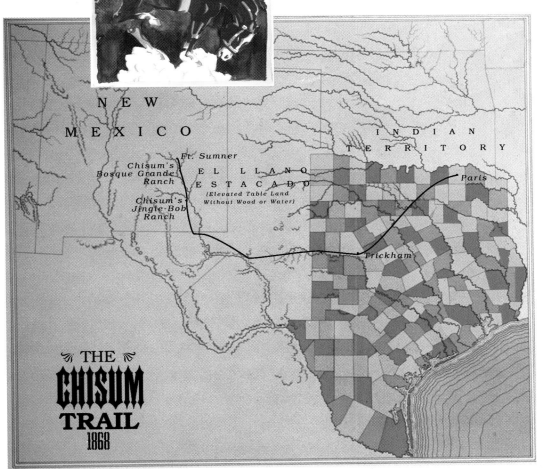

"He came with ten thousand cattle and an entourage of bronzed and weather-beaten riders of the Texas pampas, a caravan of wagons, a remuda of cow ponies, and all the dust and thunder and pomp and panoply of a royal frontier progress."

–WALTER NOBLE BURNS

SILVER CITY

THE GRANDEST COUNTRY!

THE PUREST ATMOSPHERE!
NO PEN CAN DO IT JUSTICE!

RUSH! HURRY!
DON'T WAIT FOR ANYTHING!

"YOU'LL FEEL RICHER, BETTER, MORE MILLIONAIRISH THAN ANY POOR DELUDED MORTALS EVER DID BEFORE!"

The unique atmospheric qualities of the air in **SILVER CITY** gives residents a new lease on life. Physicians claim that the magical air in the mountains of New Mexico, actually relieves pressure, and causes the blood to flow freely to the surface, thereby opening any obstruction in the capillaries equalizing the circulation of the blood.

The situation of **SILVER CITY** is such as scarcely to admit a doubt of its becoming in a short time a large and important place.

A modern, "American" city is on the march and medical doctors everywhere are extolling its virtues: to wit; countless, former citizens of the eastern states are reporting remarkable recoveries from the following troubles: torpid liver, dyspepsia, epilepsy, fits, spinal afflictions, incipient consumption, chronic rheumatism, typhoid pneumonia, and general debility.

COME ONE! COME ALL!

Inquiries addressed to either Silver City or Santa Fe will receive prompt attention

RESPONSIBLE AGENTS SOLICITED

A GOLDEN OPPORTUNITY

Late March, 1873

The Antrims find Silver City, New Mexico territory, to be a "modern American boomtown." Unlike Santa Fe and the villages along the Rio Grande with their flat-roofed adobes and narrow streets, their new home boasts a rapidly growing skyline of pitched roofs and red brick facades. And, more importantly, at 6,000 feet, Silver City and its "unique atmospheric qualities" appear to be helping Catherine's lung condition.

The newcomers establish themselves in a log cabin at the end of the "Big Ditch," the creek bed that cuts across the main street.

Bill Antrim takes odd jobs and whenever possible, heads off into the hills to look for his personal *El Dorado.*

Catherine takes in boarders to supplement their meager income. A neighbor remembers her by saying, she was a "jolly Irish lady, full of life and mischief."

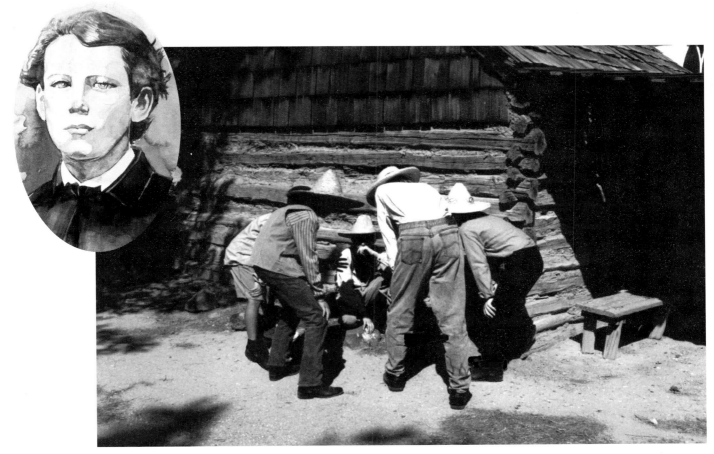

Above left, Henry on his 13th birthday, Silver City, New Mexico. Above, the Sombrero Jack gang up to no good.

Henry and his brother Josie work around the house, cleaning and cooking. They attend the new school. In later years, the Kid's teacher will give him mixed reviews: He was "a scrawny little fellow with delicate hands and an artistic nature, always willing to help with the chores around the school house. Henry was no more of a problem in school than any other boy growing up in a mining camp." The key line in the quote being, "no more of a problem than any other boy..." which, in a rough and tough mining town down on the border, leaves quite a bit of room for interpretation.

Henry joins a loose-knit gang of local boys who call themselves the Sombrero Jack gang. Their preference is the Chihuahua brand head gear. The anglo adults in the camp think they look like "a bunch of damned greasers," which of course, makes the hats that much more desirable.

The boys hang around downtown on Saturday nights and throw rocks at the drunk miners.

LINCOLN'S LEADING LIGHTS

While Billy is throwing rocks, a New Mexico community is celebrating its own.

Newlyweds Alexander and Susan McSween *have recently settled in Lincoln after a stay in Eureka, Kansas. Mrs. McSween owns the only piano in this section. Mr. McSween is a lawyer and is currently retained by L.G. Murphy and Company to make collections of House accounts.*

Juan Patrón, *To the native New Mexicans he is the guiding light in Lincoln. He is the youngest Speaker of the House in the Territorial Legislature. He owns a fully stocked store on the east side of town.*

Richard M. Brewer, *hails from Boaz, Wisconsin. A blond-haired, blue-eyed gentle giant with "great arms and huge, strong hands," Richard was known as the most powerful man in Dayton township. He is a farmer on the Ruidoso River.*

L. G. Murphy & Company: *Lincoln County's largest civilian store has been built and is operated by these fine men. Standing, left to right: "Jimmy" J. Dolan, bookkeeper; W. W. Martin, clerk. Seated, left to right: partners Col. Emil Fritz; Maj. Lawrence G. Murphy.*

Sheriff William Brady

Born August 16, 1829 in Covan, Ireland. In addition to a long and commendable career in the United States Army, Mr. Brady has spent the last few years as our able-bodied sheriff. Previously, Mr. Brady represented Lincoln County in the State House of Representatives. He became a Mason, joining the Montezuma Lodge on January 20, 1872. He owns a thousand-acre ranch four miles east of Lincoln.

Boys will be boys: *No doubt the boys are proud of their new checks recently printed in Santa Fe. We couldn't help but notice the humorous choice of a logo– Lambs lying down!*

September 16, 1874

Silver City is not the cure. Catherine McCarty is laid to rest in the town cemetery. She has been bedridden for four months.

After his mother's death, Henry works in the Knight butcher shop and boards in Richard Knight's home. Later, Henry and his brother are left in the care of the Truesdell family, who own the Star Hotel in Silver City. Henry is employed as a busboy, washing dishes and bussing tables. It is very hard to imagine some diner in the Star Hotel looking into the kitchen and remarking, "Why, look there. If it isn't the biggest folk-hero ever to come out of the Southwest!"

September, 1875

He is caught stealing several pounds of butter from a ranchman named Webb and selling it to

"Henry was the only kid who ever worked there who never stole anything. Other fellows used to steal the silverware– that kind of stuff was scarce in the camp."

–Mr. Del Truesdell
Operator of the Star Hotel

William Antrim, center, spent months at a time away from his step-children and Silver City. There is a story that the Kid had the same first two names as his step-father – William Henry. After Antrim's marriage to Catherine, the boy was called by his middle name, Henry, which he detested.

"He was a good kid but he got into the wrong company."

– LOUIS ABRAHAM

a local merchant. Billy is let off after he promises to be good.

September 23, 1875

Charming Billy, arrested for the second time, talks Sheriff Whitehill into letting him have the run of the corridor outside his cell in the converted log cabin jail.

The Sheriff leaves the boy unguarded for half an hour. "When we returned, and unlocked the heavy oaken doors of the jail, the 'Kid' was nowhere to be seen."

September 25, 1875

The local newspaper tells the story:

"Henry McCarty, who was arrested on Thursday and committed to jail to await the action of the grand jury, upon the charge of stealing clothes from Charley Sun and Sam Chung, celestials, sans cue, sans Joss sticks, escaped from prison yester-day through the chimney. It's believed that Henry was simply the tool of 'Sombrero Jack,' who done the stealing whilst Henry done the hiding. Jack skinned out."

Fifteen-year-old Henry skins out also – destination – Arizona territory.

Sheriff Harvey Whitehill and the Kid.

John Tunstall had this photo taken in San Francisco shortly after his arrival.

Below, Eadweard Muybridge's fantastic 360° photo of San Francisco in 1876 shows the Golden Gate metropolis in all its glory. It was one of the most modern cities on earth boasting such modern conveniences as cable cars, hot and cold running water, indoor bathrooms, and elevators.

Yours Till Death
John

ENTER THE ENGLISHMAN

He is short, pompous, rheumatoid, asthmatic, blind in one eye, in love with his sister, fluent in French and passable in German, and extremely patronizing towards Americans. In other words, he is your average Brit visiting the United States.

John Henry Tunstall wants to get rich quick. The 24 year-old native of London has been out west for three years working in his father's mercantile business on Vancouver Island, B.C. It hasn't gone well. According to one of his father's partners, John Turner, the young Tunstall is rude and condescending to customers. Turner's wife can't stand him either.

He will show them! Armed with letters of introduction and an advance of cash from the "Governor" (Papa Tunstall), John Henry sets sail for San Francisco.

GO EAST YOUNG MAN

As Tunstall researches his plan to buy land and raise sheep in California, he keeps getting the same message: "Too late sir! Too late sir! ...California is quite full! If you had capital to invest in it six years ago, you could have secured your run, made a pile out of sheep, & sold every acre you bought for $1.00 for $8.00 and lived independently all the rest of your life."

"The Governor"
John Partridge Tunstall

John Henry, in a letter to his father in London, states his goals," my desire is for wealth, that I may have the means of smoothing the path of life for Old

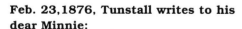

Feb. 23, 1876, Tunstall writes to his dear Minnie:

"I reached the Palace Hotel...a new hotel & the finest I ever saw; its name is very appropriate. The bed room I have is fitted with a bath room & water closet (which one can have the use of or not, according to one's purse) attached, as have all the bedrooms in the Hotel. The bed is concealed all day by folding doors; the wash stand is a picture (also concealed) fitted with hot & cold water & of marble; marble looking glass & chandeliers abound in every direction; and the table is sumtiously supplied..."

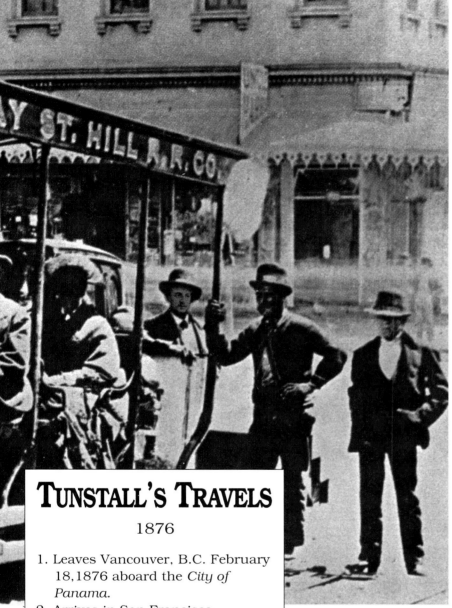

Min & our two pets..." Min refers to his sister, Minnie, with whom he made a vow years ago to take care of.

Tunstall finds all the wealthy Californios pointing him in the same direction–*east.* "The rise in property in New Mexico is quite inevitable," Mr. Cooper of Santa Rosa tells him," & that ten years will make a fortune there for any man who has a little capital, & is not afraid to invest it now."

He travels by packet to Santa Barbara and writes to Minnie that "...New Mexico will offer...as fine a field as we can wish for." He adds, "The town of Santa Barbara is not interesting though the climate is lovely."

Stating emphatically that he "would not go into partnership with the smartest man in the world," Tunstall sets off by train for New Mexico.

He arrives at Santa Fe on Tuesday, August 15,1876, and writes to his family that "everything here is in a very crude state, adobe houses with mud roofs, cattle do all the hauling & freighting, horses are very scarce & mules and donkeys very much used. The meals on the road were execrable & a dollar each."

TUNSTALL'S TRAVELS

1876

1. Leaves Vancouver, B.C. February 18,1876 aboard the *City of Panama.*
2. Arrives in San Francisco February 21, 1876.
3. March 3, 1876 takes the coastal packet *Mohango* to Santa Barbara.
4. Leaves San Francisco on August 8, 1876 on Union Pacific train.
5. Three and one-half days to Cheyenne with 15 hour layover.
6. Four hour trip to Denver.
7. 14 hour trip from Denver to El Moro (train tracks end here).
8. After a 168 hour trip, Tunstall arrives in Santa Fe August 15, 1876.

Above, Tunstall (third from right) takes in the sights of Frisco riding the Clay street trolley. Below, John dines at the famous Cliff house restaurant.

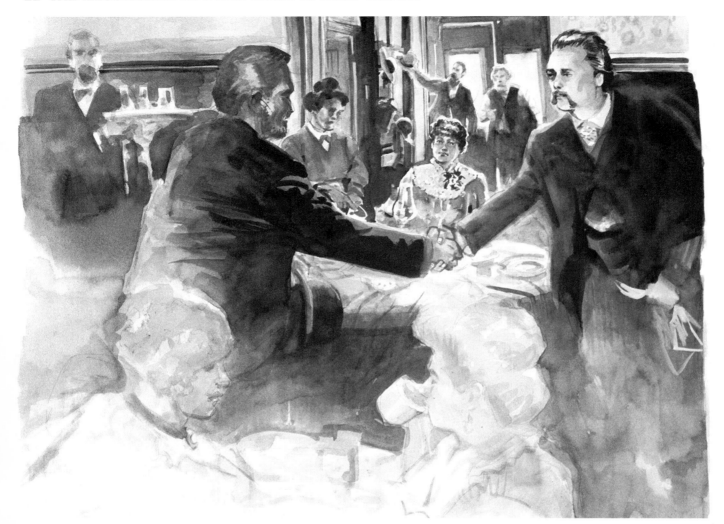

THE HANDSHAKE
FROM HELL

October 29, 1876

Two strangers meet in the dining room of the Herlow Hotel, right. John Henry Tunstall and Alexander McSween hit it off immediately. Within days, Tunstall is on his way to look over the Lincoln area. He is about to break the three rules he had set for himself: that he would not take a partner, that he would only invest in sheep, and that he would not allow ruffians to intimidate him.

CHILE AMBUSH

Like all first-time visitors to New Mexico, Tunstall no doubt had his first encounter with Mexican food similar to the one here:

"Upon the lonely looking table was only a cup of coffee, a dry tortilla (the everlasting unleavened cakes, cooked on a hot stone), and a smoking platter of apparent stewed tomatoes. Now if there is anything which does not appeal to my stomach it is stewed tomatoes; but I was too hungry to be fastidious. There was nothing wherewith to eat except an enormous iron spoon, and with starving and unseemly haste I ladled a liberal supply from the platter to my plate and swallowed the first big spoonful at a gulp. And then I sprang up with a howl of pain and terror, fully convinced that these "treacherous Mexicans" had assassinated me by quick poison–for I had very ignorant and silly notions in those days about Mexicans, as most of us are taught by superficial travellers who do not know one of the kindliest races in the world. My mouth and throat were consumed with living fire, and my stomach was a pit of boiling torture. I snatched the cup of hot coffee and swallowed half its contents–which aggravated my distress ten-fold, as any of you will understand who may try the experiment. I rushed from the house and plunged into a snowbank, biting the snow to quench that horrible inner fire... Poison? No, indeed, señor. That was only *chile colorado, chile con carne,* which is liked to the Mexicans *mucho*–and to many Americanos–*tambien.*"

– CHARLES F. LUMMIS
1884, CARNOE, NEW MEXICO

In a letter home Tunstall describes meeting McSween: "There is a very nice young fellow here just now from Lincoln County, a lawyer by profession, who has the outward appearance of an honest man, (Herlow speaks very highly of him) he has been trying to persuade me to go into stock & not buy land but I have seen too much of California to do so unless I am obliged. But I must say that his plan has a great deal to recommend it."

November 16, 1876

Tunstall writes to his "Much Beloved Trinity" about his trip to Lincoln: "It was snowing... the roads were like pudding... our horses were a couple of poor scarecrows... Patrón... flogged his horses along... he never availed himself of the solid parts of the road, but went right along in the ruts & mud... his reins always hung down... on unharnessing the team I accidentally let the sound horse loose & it took us about an hour to catch him... The next day the roads were worse..."

On reaching Lincoln he says, "Placita consists of a small collection of adobe house scattered up a pretty creek called the Rio Bonita (which means Pretty River) & in miner's parlance about the "toughest" little spot in America, which means the most lawless."

After spending the night at Juan Patrón's, he writes, "I called on Mrs. McSween & found her a very pleasant woman in every way, she told me as much about the place as any man could have done, she is the only white woman here & has a good many enemies in consequence of her husband's profession."

January 1, 1876

Jesse Evans, John Kinney and others kill two soldiers and a civilian at a dance in Las Cruces.

January 12, 1876

John Chisum and attorney Thomas Conway are robbed while riding on a stagecoach at Cook's canyon between Silver City and Mesilla. Chisum tries to pay the thieves in cattle but they refuse.

February 5, 1876

Susan McSween hires Francisco Gomez to help move some furniture. Afterwards, she coaxes him out by the banks of the Bonito for a little "Spanish lesson."

February 14, 1876

Inventors Alexander Graham Bell and Elisha Gray apply separately for patents related to the telephone. The U.S. Supreme Court eventually rules Bell (no relation) the rightful inventor.

March 11, 1876

Francisco Gomez corners Susan McSween in the rear kitchen. She whispers "si" many times.

August 8, 1876

Thomas Edison receives a patent for the mimeograph.

August 23, 1876

While visiting the Chisum ranch, Susan McSween offers John Chisum a Spanish lesson. Hungry for knowledge, he accepts.

October 17, 1876

While looking at Spanish land grants Tunstall comments, "Spanish people who have any regard for themselves never leave their daughters five minutes alone with any gentleman for reasons best known to themselves."

WHAT THINGS COST
1880 PRICES

A Colt .45 costs $12.

A box of shells, 50 cents.

A Winchester, model 1873 costs $24.

A steer costs $9.

A cow with its calf, $16.50.

A meal at a train station, $1.

A pair of Levis, $1.46.

A newspaper subscription to the Deming Headlight, $3 a year in advance, circulation 200. Price of advertising, seven inches three months, $25. The printing press costs $25.

A weeks board at a rooming house, $6.

A bushel of potatoes, $3.25.

A stick of butter, 45 cents.

A railroad tie, 55 cents.

A store 25′ X 60′ on main street in Socorro rents for $80 to $100 a month.

A bank loans money at 18 percent.

A city lot in Albuquerque, $100.

A salesman in a store is paid $50 to $150 a month.

A room at the Palace Hotel in Santa Fe costs $4 a day.

A "dance" license for saloons in Las Vegas, N.M. costs $5 per evening.

A quart of beer, 15 cents.

Gus Gildea

"He came to town dressed like a country jake with shoes instead of boots. He wore a six-gun stuck in his trousers."

– GUS GILDEA

BILLY IN ARIZONA

September 26,1875

The Kid crosses the border into Arizona territory. He shows up at a hay camp at Camp Thomas and asks for work. J.W. "Sorghum" Smith recalled," He said he was 17 though he didn't look to be 14."

Kid Antrim, age 16

He spends nearly two years in Arizona but few of his activities are documented. Legend and folklore have filled the gaps. To hear tell, every rancher in southeastern Arizona hid him and every other old-timer saw Billy the Kid shooting his way across the landscape. Truth is he was just an unemployed busboy named William Henry Antrim.

Mount Graham

Camp Grant

Hotel De Luna

Atkins Saloon

SULPHUR SPRINGS VALLEY

SADDLE BANDITS

Billy and an accomplice named Mackie begin stealing saddles around the Camp Grant area to make money. The price of a new saddle ranges from $30 (a month's wage for a cowboy) to $150.

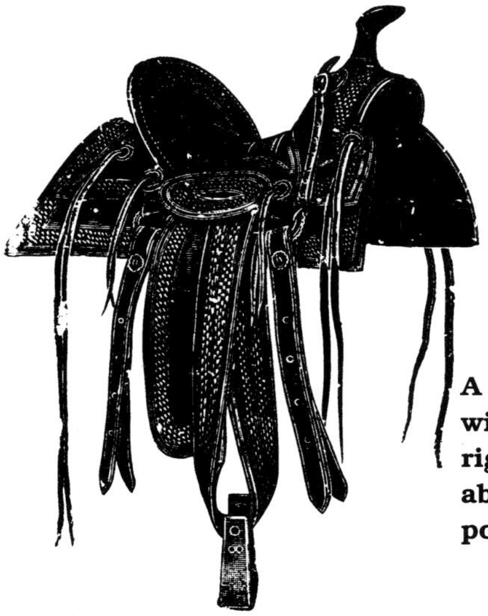

A Texas saddle with full rigging weighs about 40 pounds.

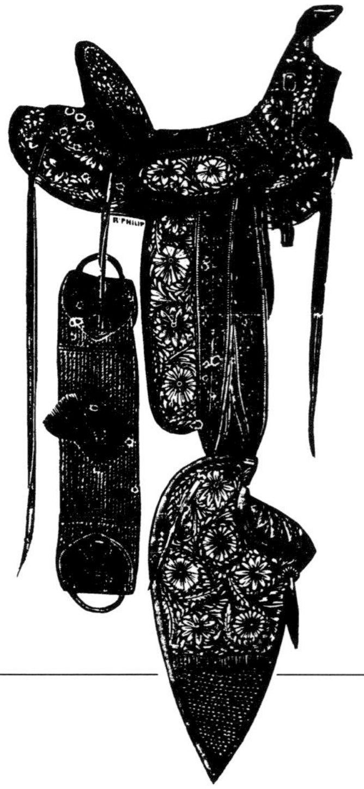

A Mexican saddle with 24" tapaderas (leather casings to protect the rider's feet from cacti)

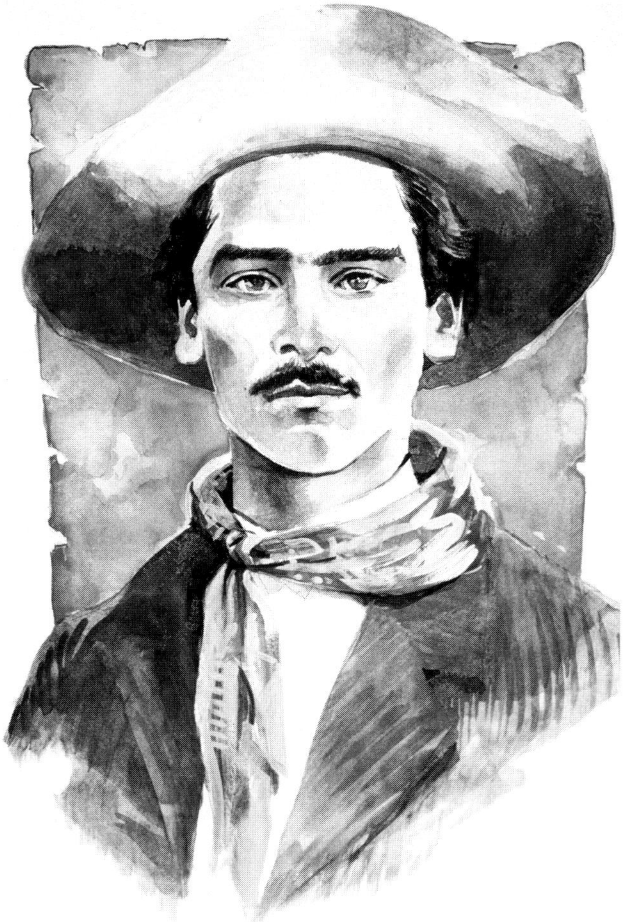

William Whelan, the Hooker Ranch general manager, hired Billy but let him go because he couldn't "stand the gaff."

"We take a man here and ask no questions. We know when he throws a saddle on his horse whether he understands his business or not. He may be a minister back-slidin', or a banker savin' his last lung, or a train robber on a vacation – we don't care. A good many of our most useful men have made their mistakes. All we care about is, will they stand the gaff? Will they sit sixty hours in the saddle, holdin' a herd that's tryin' to stampede all the time?"

–HENRY CLAY HOOKER

Hotel De Luna

BILLY IN BONITA

BILLY THE KID ★ BONITA, ARIZONA

August 17th, 1877.

1877

Billy lands a job cooking and busing tables at the Hotel de Luna near Camp Grant. He falls in with an ex-soldier named John R. Mackie and the two begin stealing horses and saddles. Miles Woods, the owner of the Hotel de Luna and the local justice of the peace, recalls a particular event in which the Kid and his partner crowned their horse-theft adventures:

"A lieutenant and a doctor came down one day. They said they would fix it so that no one would steal their horses. They had long picket ropes on the horses and when they went into the bar, carried the ropes with them. Mackie talked to the officers quite a while and when they came out they only had a piece of rope in their hands. The Kid had gone with the horses."

July, 1877

Not long after the picket-rope affair, Miles Wood saw the Kid and Mackie enter the hotel for breakfast. "I told the waiter that I would wait on them. I took a large server tray and took it in and slipped it on the table in front of them. Pulled a six-gun from under it and told them 'hands up.'"

Wood walked them out the door and herded them on foot the 2½ miles to the guardhouse at Camp Grant.

About an hour after the Kid was locked up, he asked the sergent of the guard to take him out for some purpose. Wood noted in his reminiscences:

"Right back of the guardhouse, and in front of several men, the Kid turned and threw a handful of salt in the guard's eyes and grabbed his gun." But the attempt failed. The guard yelled for help, and the men disarmed the boy

and returned him to confinement. Wood, who had walked back to his hotel, was summoned back to the camp where he had the blacksmith fit the Kid with a pair of shackles riveted around his ankles. But it was to do little good.

"That night," Wood wrote, "myself and my wife were at a reception at the colonel's house when the sergeant of the guard came to the door and called the colonel out. In a few minutes, he came back and said the Kid was gone, shackles and all."

Miles Wood herded Billy and Mackie up this road to Camp Grant.

THE CITIZEN

SATURDAY,   AUGUST 25, 1877

LOCAL MATTERS

Probate Court Matters.

Hon. J. S. Wood, judge and B. H. Hereford, clerk. During the week cases were heard and passed upon, to wit;

AUSTIN ANTRIM shot F. B. Cahill near Camp Grant on the 17th instant, and latter died on the 18th. Cahill made a statement before death to the effect that he had some trouble with Antrim during which the shooting was done. Bad names were applied each to the other. Deceased has a sister – Margaret Flanegan in Cambridge, Mass., and another – Kate Conlon in San Francisco. He was born in Galway, Ireland, and was aged about 32. The coroner's jury found that the shooting "was criminal and unjustifiable, and that "Henry Antrim, alias Kid, is guilty there- "of." The inquest was held by M. L. Wood, J. P., and the jurors were M. McDowell, Geo. Teague, T. McCleary, B. E. Norton, Jas. L. Hunt and D. H. Smith.

"I called him a pimp, and he called me a sonofabitch," Cahill told bystanders before he died. The newspaper got his name wrong but it doesn't matter. From now on, he has a new alias – Billy Bonney. The Kid flees, never to return to Arizona.

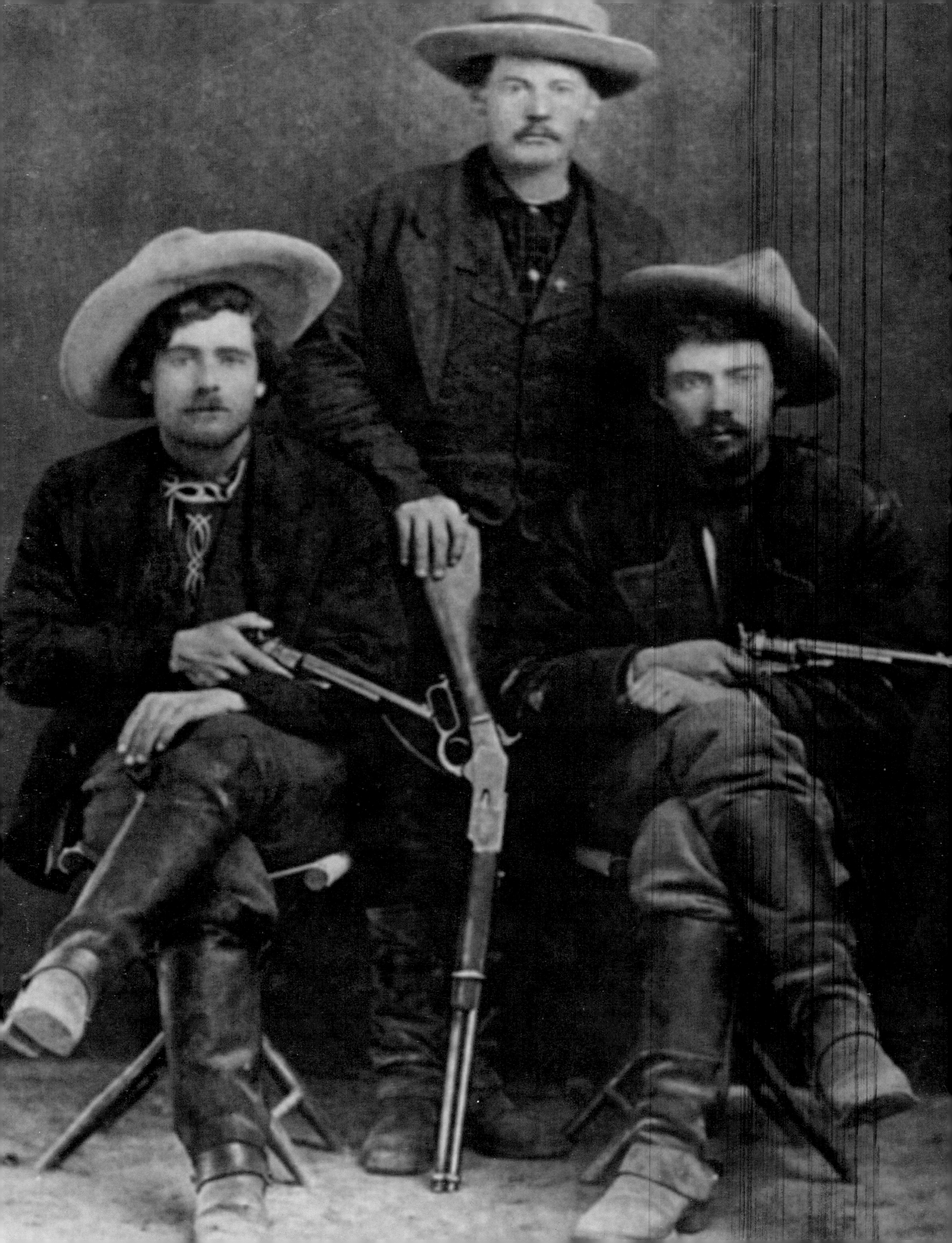

*"We was all just a
bunch of wild kids."*

–ADD CASEY

John Kinney, left center, and his
two outlaw lieutenants center their
operations in the Mesilla Valley. His
ranch is described in a local newspaper as "the headquarters and
rendezvous for all the evil doers in
the county." Meanwhile, Jesse
Evans and his gang are spotted at
the Pass Coal Camp. Identified
among the bandits is Billy Bonney.
As Evans and company make their
way from Silver City to Las Cruces,
they eat and drink plenty and tell
all the proprietors to "chalk it up."

He never seemed to care for money, except to buy cartridges with; then he would much prefer to gamble for them straight. Cartridges were scarce, and he always used about 10 times as many as any one else.

—FRANK B. COE

"There wasn't much entertainment those days except to hunt."

—FRANK B. COE

Billy Bonney Bags a Bear, left to right, The Kid, George Coe, Dead Bear, Frank Coe.

Frank Coe, San Patricio, 1877

"I've ridden weary miles with him; I've starved and faced the bars with him, and I've played the fiddle when he danced, while a sergeant and a deputy sat in the room with orders to arrest him, dead or alive."

—FRANK COE

Desert Dance Floor Maintenance

During "Storm" dances when the adobe ranch house dirt floors got to clouding up the room, the host would grab a shovel and put it in the fireplace until it heated up and then repack the floor for another round.

Winter, 1877

Sometime in October or early November, Billy lands in Lincoln County. The Jones family, of Seven Rivers, says he showed up at their place on Rocky Arroyo one day, on foot, sore and hungry.

Mrs. Barbara Culp Jones, or Ma'am Jones as she was called, remembers finding the boy outside her ranch house, wearing no socks and with raw and swollen feet. He tells her he hasn't eaten in three days. She heats some milk.

"I don't like milk," he tells her.

Ma'am Jones has ten kids – nine of them boys, "Do you want me to hold your nose and pour it down you?"

The Kid wisely drinks the milk, recovers, and borrowing a horse, heads up into the Sacramentos.

The Coes claim Billy spends a good part of the winter with them, hunting and dancing. He is adept at both.

WAR CLOUDS

Jimmy Dolan became a partner in L. G. Murphy & Co. on April 1, 1874. He had worked his way up from bookkeeper and his mentor, Murphy, thought he was ready. Actually, Murphy had been rapidly declining in health due to his massive drinking habit.

Finally, Murphy withdraws completely from the business on March 14, 1877.

April 3, 1877

Smallpox kills Mescalero Apache chiefs Roman, Pinole and Greely.

April 12,1877

The catcher's mask is first used in a baseball game.

Spring, 1877

Dolan takes a new partner,

Two peas in a pod: Jimmy Dolan learned everything he knows from his mentor, Lawrence G. Murphy. Both are ex-military and ruthless. But now, Murphy has decided to quit the business. His drinking has all but incapacitated him. Dolan will do him proud.

"Murphy was never married, but he always kept a Mexican woman that came from the high class. He could drink and walk under more whiskey than any man I saw."
–FRANK COE

"An Irish homosexual is a man who prefers women to drink."

"Kid" Antrim is now going by another alias, William H. Bonney.

John Riley, a man he tried to shoot during a church service at Fort Stanton several years prior. The new partners style their business as J. J. Dolan & Co. and together they hope to continue their sweet monopoly.

Just down the street from the House, two other men hope to create their own sweet monopoly. John Tunstall and Alexander McSween feel they have the cards to beat the House. First of all, McSween has seen their books and knows what a fine mess they've made. Second of all, they feel smarter and morally superior to the "Micks." And most of all, they are both greedy, educated and on the make – in a later time they would be called Frontier Yuppies.

Billy Bonney is well known to both parties. They attend the same dances and social events. In fact "there wasn't enough of Billy to go around," Frank Coe said.

According to legend, Tunstall took a liking to the boy and took him under his wing. He may have, but in all the letters to his "Pets" in England, John never mentions the Kid once. By contrast, Tunstall goes on and on about

Rob Widenmann until one wants to hurl.

October, 1877

Things are getting complicated. Col. Fritz, Murphys original business partner, had gone home to Germany and died on June 26, 1874. Prior to his departure, Fritz had taken out a life insurance policy for $10,000 in favor of the beneficiaries of his estate. A year later, after the insurance company had not paid, Murphy brought the matter to McSween for collection.

Receiving a power of attorney from Mrs. Emile Fritz Scholand and Charles Fritz, administrators of the estate, McSween travelled to New York in October, 1876 (he was en route when he met Tunstall at the Herlow Hotel in Santa Fe).

Even though the insurance company had gone into receivership, McSween retained a New York financial firm to help him collect. Lo and behold, they did. On August 1, 1877 Donnell, Lawson & Co. credited McSween's account with $7,148.94.

Back in Lincoln, as soon as Dolan hears, he claims the money is owed by Fritz to the firm.

McSween refuses to give up the money. His wife also begins to remodel the house. Francisco Gomez starts taking thorough measurements in the bedroom.

December 21, 1877

Dolan rides to La Mesilla and gets a charge of embezzlement against McSween.

December 24, 1877

McSween and Chisum are "detained" at Las Vegas pending arrival of warrant. Mrs. McSween continues on to St. Louis.

FRONTIER SLANG

A running pass at everyday language out in the wilds of New Mexico territory

Housed up: What happens to residents when cowboys start shooting up the town.

Long-headed: Somebody with ample brains. A horse is considered more intelligent if he's "long-headed."

Spunk up: get courage, as in "Why don't you spunk up and ask that girl to dance?"

Gabble: Useless talk, as in "I paid no attention to their senseless gabble."

Hived: Refers to humans being trapped like bees, as in "The Kid and his gang were hived."

Curled darlings: Members of high society, a contemptuous term.

Dead head ticket: to be dead, as in "another outlaw received a dead head ticket to the happy hunting grounds; also, "Law was a dead-letter in the county."

Eat: To kill, as in "I'm fixin' to go below and eat a few Tejanos."

Jump: To surprise, as in "What do you jump us up in this style for?"

Corn: With gusto, as in "The question of surrender was discussed and vetoed by the Kid with corn."

Crack your crust: To break the skin with heavy blows, as in "I'll crack your crust!"

Lead pump: Slang for a lever-action Winchester, as in "You can't start your lead pump any too quick to suit me."

Rack out: To get your gear packed and head out, as in "Just before sunup we racked out on the road."

Hang fire: To wait, as in "I refused to die, so they had to hang fire until I could be moved."

Jacking up: To cuss someone out, as in "I caught a good jacking up from the chief boss."

The Devil's Hatband: Barbed wire.

The Edge: To get the upper hand, or gain an advantage over an opponent, as in "'New Mexico, where the edge is almighty."

Bonito Bravos, left to right, Chavez y Chavez, Francisco Gomez, and Yginio Salazar.

"New Mexico – so far from Heaven, so close to Texas."
– OLD VAQUERO SAYING

LOCOS

April 19, 1877
Tunstall receives the first draft from his father. In all he will have about $20,000 to invest.

April 24, 1877
Tunstall files on land and establishes a ranch on the Feliz river.

July 1, 1877
Rob Widenmann comes down with smallpox. Tunstall nurses him back to health.

July 7, 1877
Tunstall leaves Lincoln on buying trip to Saint Louis and Kansas City.

July 12, 1877
John Chisum starts for Arizona with 2,500 head of cattle.

July 30, 1877
Tunstall's sister marries. John, feeling betrayed becomes totally distraught. All of his efforts in New Mexico are for her. He writes her a very emotional letter, signing off, "Yours till death."

July 31, 1877
Susan McSween needs some yardwork done. She hires Francisco Gomez and shows him the area behind the stables she would like worked on.

August 11, 1877
Jesse Evans and the Boys raid the Mescalero reservation, stealing horses for John Chisum. The Apaches call them the "Big Hats." The native New Mexicans call *any* outlaw gang "Tejanos."

HEAD TO HEAD

October 29, 1877

Tunstall store opens for business with Samuel Corbet, manager and clerk. McSween (pictured above shaking hands with Tunstall) has an office in the new building and there is also a bank, right (note who the officers are).

Finally, John Henry can go head to head with the Irish crowd and show them a thing or two.

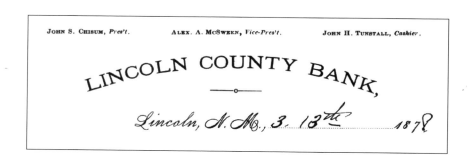

JOHN S. CHISUM, *Pres't.*   ALEX. A. McSWEEN, *Vice-Pres't.*   JOHN H. TUNSTALL, *Cashier.*

LINCOLN COUNTY BANK,

Lincoln, N. M., 3. 13th   1878

"I told Tunstall and Mr. McSween they would be murdered if they went into the store business. I did my best to keep McSween from entering the business, but he went in against my will. Tunstall was the cause of his getting into it."

—SUSAN McSWEEN

In spite of the rampant racism that seemed to infuse every level of 1800s America, there were exceptions like this cover of Harper's Weekly. The caption reads, "'EVERY DOG' (NO DISTINCTION OF COLOR) 'HAS HIS DAY.' Red Gentleman to Yellow Gentleman, 'Pale face 'fraid you crowd him out, as he did me.'"

November, 1877

"Kid" Antrim is employed by Tunstall who is paying $3 a day for "fighting men." The Kid also gets a new suit and weapons. He tells a friend that it's the first time in his life that someone, other than his mother, treated him right.

January, 1878

McSween is under house arrest for embezzlement. Bail is set for $8,000. McSween's defense is that he is holding the insurance monies until the proper people can be paid. The District Attorney refuses to accept McSween's bondsmen.

February 9, 1878

Sheriff Brady attaches McSween's property and Tunstall's because they are "partners." Tunstall denies that they are, but the Sheriff begins proceedings against him anyway and attaches the Tunstall store. Rob Widenmann, who protests, is arrested.

February 11, 1878

Tunstall sends his boys, including the Kid, to the ranch with the horses and mules exempted by Brady. It is a fifty mile ride.

February 12, 1878

A posse led by Billy Mathews goes to the Tunstall ranch on the Feliz. They want the cattle but Richard Brewer refuses to turn them over. A gunfight almost erupts when Jesse Evans and several of the Boys advance on Widenmann bringing their weapons to full cock in his face. He backs down.

February 13, 1878

The posse returns to Lincoln for further instructions. Incredibly, Widenmann, Bonney, and Waite ride along with them!

February 16, 1878

Tunstall sends his boys back to the ranch while he travels to Chisum's ranch on the Pecos, to see if he can get help. Chisum is not home and Tunstall leaves empty-handed.

TUNSTALL'S LAST RIDE

February 17, 1878

Discouraged and dog tired, Tunstall reached his ranch long past dark on the evening of February 17. He had just ridden over 100 miles in 24 hours.

His men had fortified the crude ranch house by piling up grain sacks filled with dirt and drilling port holes in the walls of the adobe dwelling. They numbered eight: Widenmann, Bonney, Brewer, Middleton, Waite, McCloskey, Gauss and Brown. All of them were ready for a fight.

John Henry immediately vetoed his warrior's plan. He repeated the course of action he had

Tunstall's "Ranch" is actually just a 14′ square log cabin with sand filled grain sacks piled in front. The sheriff's posse did an inventory of the premises and found the following: 360 head of cattle, 2 shovels and an anvil.

vowed to McSween before leaving Lincoln: "I will not sacrifice the life of a single man for all the cattle... Mathews and his crowd can take my property, and I will seek remedy in the courts."

There was a rumor that Dolan had slipped out of Lincoln and was assembling his forces at Paul's ranch, nearby. It was true. Thanks to an inside tip, Tunstall was fully informed of the activities at Paul's ranch, seven miles away, where a large force of Anglos and Mexicans had gathered. The native New Mexicans, it was reported, were to round up and drive off the cattle, while the "Big Hats" took care of the men at the ranch. Bonney figured they were outnumbered four to one. He was just about dead on.

After dinner, the besieged Englishman and his cowboys sat around the fire drinking coffee and debating Dolan's next move. Tunstall still believed he could outmaneuver Mathews, Brady and Dolan with a series of chess-like moves. Brewer, Bonney and Waite were not quite as confident as their boss. They knew the game their opponents were playing was not chess.

Tired and wired, having less than three hours sleep in the last 48 hours, Tunstall painstakingly went over his options. Finally, at about 3 a.m. he dispatched McCloskey down to the Penasco to get "Dutch" Martin, an acknowledged neutral and skilled cattle counter, to come over and tally the herd for the transfer to the posse. Then, since he had friends among the crowd at Paul's ranch, McCloskey was to ride over to Turkey Springs and inform whoever was in charge that there would be no resistance.

Satisfied that he had covered his bases as well as possible, the

Armed and Impotent

L to R; Richard Brewer (Tunstall's foreman), Fred Waite, John Middleton, Billy Bonney and Rob Widenmann line up in front of the campfire before their ill-fated ride. They all appear to sport two cartridge belts apiece (all the go during the war) and the Kid carries a long-barrel Smith & Wesson revolver in cross-draw fashion. The fact is that Billy the Kid probably carried many different weapons in his short career. Tunstall paid each of these men "fighting wages" of three dollars a day and yet not one of them fired a shot when the party was attacked.

Tunstall killed here

Lincoln

Pajarito Peak

Wagon Road

Pajarito cutoff

Lincoln Canyon

Rio Feliz

Paul's Ranch

Tunstall Ranch

Tunstall's Last Ride Ten miles ahead, Tunstall and his cowboys had already veered off to the left, driving the horses up towards the mountain trail to Pajarito Flats and on into Lincoln. It was a shortcut. An extra insurance policy against an unwanted confrontation with Mathew's men. Fred Waite, driving a buckboard, continued on the wagon road.

The pursuing posse had no trouble tracking the fourteen horses ahead of them. They easily caught the turnoff and quickly surmised Tunstall's intent. As the posse leaned into the saddle they steadily began to whittle away at the distance between them and Tunstall. By the time they passed Pajarito Springs, only a half hour separated them. Beyond Pajarito Flats the thick stands of pine and narrow trail spread out the posse along the mountain ridge.

exhausted Tunstall turned in for a few fitful hours of sleep.

At first light, the boys had the horses saddled and pointed north. The whole outfit tip-toed around the camp as they ate their breakfast, trying to give their leader a few extra minutes of shuteye. Old Gauss finally brought Tunstall a tin of hot tea and gently nudged him. It was time to go.

The Kid and John Middleton rode drag as the Tunstall party hit the trail for Lincoln. Ahead of them were nine horses; six were those released by Brady on the eleventh, two belonged to Brewer, and the last belonged to Bonney. Or more accurately, it belonged to the sheriff of Las Cruces until Billy and the Boys lifted it. And now it was this horse that furnished the pretext for Jesse Evans and the Boys continued presence with the posse.

Tunstall and Brewer rode ahead. Tunstall looked very tired. The stress of the past several months had begun to take its toll. After a mile, Henry Brown's horse threw a shoe. Unable to keep up he left the group and headed back. Incredibly enough, he exchanged greetings with the posse on its way to Tunstall's ranch from Paul's!

Back at the ranch, Old Gauss cleaned up the breakfast dishes and stoked the fire. It was a brisk New Mexico morning with temperatures in the low forties. As he rattled around the camp, the posse made a wary approach from two directions. Finally satisfied it wasn't a trap, the Dolan party poured into the yard, surrounding the lone cook. Spoiling for a fight, more than a few of the posse members were vastly disappointed that conditions were just as McCloskey had stated.

Jimmy Dolan quickly conferred with Mathews and Billy Morton. They confronted Gauss. Where were the horses? The posse, they informed the old man, wasn't satisfied with just the cattle. Gauss played dumb, but Henry Brown's hobbling horse would point the way.

Mathews designated fourteen men and deputized Billy Morton, Dolan's cow camp boss, to lead a chase after Tunstall to retrieve the horses.

Jesse Evans made ready to join them along with his compadres, Frank Baker and Tom Hill.

Mathews objected mildly, but Evans declared that he and his men had a right to go after their own property, that the Kid had their "horses" and they intended to get them back.

Gauss said he gave them something to eat, or rather, "they helped themselves to what they wanted."

Mathews then said to him, "Why didn't someone remain to turn over the property?"

Gauss told him Mertz would be there to do that. "They then commenced shoeing their horses out of Tunstall's property: three or four horses were shod."

As the sub-posse saddled up, Gauss heard Billy Morton cry out, "Hurry up, boys, my knife is sharp, and I feel like scalping some one."

Pantaleon Gallegos started to make a list of the posse; when he saw that Gallegos was writing down the names of Evans, Baker, Hill, and Davis, Mathews spoke to him sharply and said, "Don't put them boys down at all."

Tunstall's party had about an hour and one-half head start. As the seventeen man posse thundered up the draw north of the

Jimmy Dolan (seated) called all the shots in the tragic events unfolding on these pages. He is seen here in this photo with Robert Olinger, who rode in the first posse. Robert figures prominently in the last phase of Billy the Kid's life.

ranch, Gauss noted, "They were all excited and seemed as though they were agoing to kill someone."

The leaders, Evans, Morton and Hill stopped only to take a pull on a flask. Their horses lathered and wet, they pushed on until there was over a mile between the front of the posse to the back.

Late afternoon light began to tip the tops of the foothills leading down into the Ruidoso Valley. As the Tunstall party crested a divide and started down a narrow gorge leading to the river. They had been in the saddle for over nine hours and were less than ten minutes from Brewer's farm.

The Kid and Middleton continued to ride drag, pushing the horses towards the Ruidoso. Ahead, the main group, consisting of Tunstall, Widenmann and Brewer scared up a flock of wild turkeys. Widenmann and Brewer took off in pursuit. Totally fatigued and his mind no doubt many miles away, Tunstall remained ahead of the horses as he descended deeper into the draw.

Just as they topped the divide with the horses, Billy Bonney and John Middleton glimpsed a group of horsemen galloping up the trail behind them. Spurring their mounts, the two scattered the remuda as they ran through the herd to alert their compadres.

Shouting and waving, Billy was about half way to Widenmann and Brewer when the pursuers cleared the brow of the divide. Spotting the three men to their left front, the posse leaders opened fire. Bullets cracked between them and sent Brewer's horse bucking. Caught in the open on a treeless slope, all three headed for a hilltop strewn with boulders.

Middleton, aboard his bay, had reached Tunstall just as the

shooting started. They both turned in the saddle to see the first of three posse members clear the crest and open fire with their Winchesters on Billy, Dick and Rob.

Middleton said he "Sung out to Tunstall to follow me. He was on a

good horse; he appeared to be very much excited and confused. I kept singing out to him "For God's sake, follow me." His last words were, "What, John? What, John?"

Seeing Tunstall, the posse gave up their attack on Billy and the boys and turned down the hill towards the "Englishman."

Middleton peeled off from Tunstall and quickly made his way up the side of the ravine to the defensive position taken by Bonney, Brewer and Widenman. As he dismounted, they heard a burst of gunfire echo down through the canyon. John said out loud what all four were thinking, "They've killed Tunstall."

February 18, 1878

Ramon Baragon found the body. Brewer and his men had stopped at John Newcomb's farm on the Ruidoso with instructions to bring Tunstall's body into Lincoln.

Baragon and the search party found him "lying closely by the side of his horse." Florencio Gonzales reported that "Tunstall's overcoat was placed under his head, and his hat placed under the head of his dead horse. By the apparent naturalness of the scene we were forced to conclude that the murderers of Mr. Tunstall placed his dead horse in the position indicated, considering the whole affair a burlesque."

Forty armed men were waiting at McSween's when they brought the body in strapped to a donkey. In addition to his wounds, his face and legs were scraped from the ride over the mountain trail.

Dr. Taylor Ealy described the scene, "We found ourselves in the center of a battlefield – about 40 men armed in full fighting trim – double belts of cartridges, one for the revolvers and the other for the Winchester rifles."

The body was laid out on a table in a back room of the Tunstall store. "Kid walked up," Frank Coe related, "looked at him, and said, 'I'll get some of them before I die,' and turned away."

BILLY'S FAVORITE SPANISH QUOTES

De la carcel sales pero de la tumba no.
Men walk out of jail but never from the tomb.

Dinero atrae dinero.
Money attracts money.

El que mal anda mal acaba.
He who walks in evil ends in evil.

Escupe en el cielo y regresara.
Spit in the sky and it comes back.

Gente que tienen lo que quieren encontraron la manera de decir a Gente que no tienen lo que quieren lo que ellos ver daderamente no quieren.
People who have what they want are fond of telling people who haven't what they want that they really don't want it.

El trabajo es el progreso del hombre.
Work is the means by which a man progresses.

Es mejor dar que recibir.
It is better to give than to receive.

Paras una madre no hay mal hijo.
To a mother a bad son does not exist.

Vive despacio y duraras mas años.
Pace yourself and you will live a longer life.

El quke a hierro mata a jierro muere.
He who kills with a weapon dies by a weapon.

De mejores partes me han corrido y me he ido.
From better places I have been thrown out and gone.

El que nace para tamal, del cielo le caen las hojas.
He who is destined to be a tamale will find corn shucks falling from the sky.

Si los borrachos tuvieran alas, estuviera el cielo nublado.
If drunks had wings, the sky would always be cloudy.

Viendo caballo ensillado se les ofrece viaje.
The man who sees a saddled horse often decides he needs to take a trip.

¡Ni por relajo!
Not by a damn sight!

El valiente vive hasta que el cobarde quiera.
The brave man lives only as long as the coward allows him.

BRADY GETS TOUGH

February, 19,1878

Constable Atanacio Martinez, with Kid Bonney and Fred Waite along as deputies, goes to the Dolan store to arrest the men named in warrants for the murder of John Tunstall. The trio encounters a heavily armed group of Dolan men inside the store, including William Brady. The Sheriff not only refuses to let Martinez make any arrests, but places the three under arrest, disarms them, and marches them down the street to the jail in full sight of the entire town. Martinez is eventually released but the Kid and Waite are kept in the hole. The humiliation of this act will cost the sheriff of Lincoln County dearly.

THE STORM AFTER THE STORM

It's business.
It's class.
It's religion.
It's ethnic.
But most of all,
it's about to
get personal.

Monday, April 1, 1878.

Sheriff Brady comes into Lincoln from his farm east of town.

He has breakfast at the Wortley Hotel and then crosses the street to the House. He is met there at 9 a.m. by George Hindman, Billy Mathews, George Peppin and John Long. All five are armed with repeating rifles. The Sheriff carries a Winchester '73 which he took off of William Bonney on February 20.

The heavy rains have left the ground soggy and the men pick their way around the bogs as they walk east down the main street of Lincoln.

Brady stops momentarily to say something to Mrs. Ham Mills who is in her yard. Both of them laugh at his corny joke. It is April Fools' Day.

APRIL FOOLS' AMBUSH
1878

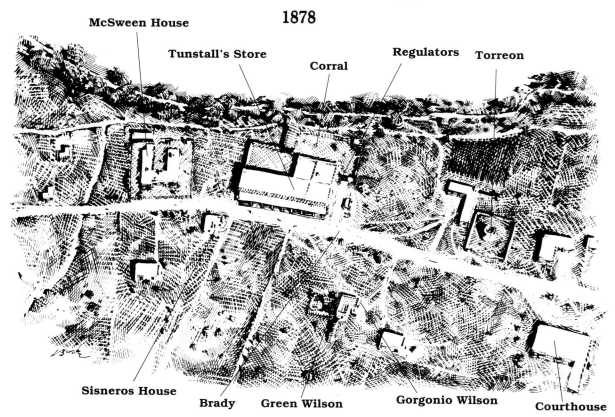

McSween House

Tunstall's Store

Regulators

Torreon

Corral

Sisneros House

Brady

Green Wilson

Gorgonio Wilson

Courthouse

From across the street, Dr. Taylor F. Ealy sees the exchange and watches as Brady hurries to catch up with his posse.

As the quintet clears the southeast corner of the Tunstall store, a storm of bullets sweep the street. Shooting from behind makeshift portals carved into the high adobe walls of the corral, the concealed gunmen strike down Brady and Hindman. The Sheriff is hit by no less than 12 balls.

Across the road and catty corner from the store, Gorgonio Wilson, 6, is playing in the yard with his sister Junita when they hear loud explosions. He looks up to see Mr. Brady fall to a sitting position. Gorgonio watches in horror as he tries to get up. Brady cries out, "Oh Lord," and then another round of shots riddles his body and he falls backwards, dead.

Gorgonio's father, Squire Wilson, is in the backyard hoeing onions. He lets out a moan and falls forward, having been hit by a stray bullet that passes through his buttocks.

Incredibly, George Hindman is moving. He cries out for water. Ike Stockton emerges from his saloon, rushes into the street and attempts to pull the wounded man to safety. As he is being led off the battlefield another bullet drops the deputy, ending his life.

During the first volley, Mathews, Peppin and Long scattered and quickly ran back to the Sisneros house, taking cover in the front room. Long is hit, but Mathews and Peppin have miraculously ran through a curtain of lead, untouched.

"When he was rough, he was as rough as men ever get to be."

¬JOHN MEADOWS

For a long pregnant pause, the street is completely quiet except for the barking of dogs down the street. There is talking behind the adobe wall. Two men leap the corral wall and sprint into the street. It is "Big Jim" French and Billy Bonney. Covered by French, the Kid stoops over Brady and picks up his Winchester and starts to reach into the Sheriff's vest.

Billy Mathews, peeking through the window of the Cisneros house, takes aim and fires.

The bullet clips Billy's hip and rips through Big Jim's thigh. Bonney drops his rifle and the two hot foot it back to the safety of the corral.

Rob Widenmann opens the north gate of the corral and all the regulators mount up except for French, who can't get his leg over the saddle.

Mathews, Peppin and Long hear the horses thunder out of the corral heading east along the Bonito, out of sight. The three carefully leave the safety of the Cisneros front room and peer down the street to see the Regulators rejoin the road just west of the Ellis store. The deputies dash into the street and begin firing at the escaping assassins.

As the Regulators gallop out of range, John Middleton cooly stops his horse, dismounts, sits down and, resting his elbow on his knee, fires back at the rattled deputies.

They scatter.

THOSE WHO KNEW BILLY THE KID DESCRIBE HIM...

"He had the face of an angel, the soft voice of a woman, and the mild blue eyes of a poet."
–Yginio Salazar
Fought with Billy in Lincoln County war

"...he weighed about 125 pounds and was five feet seven inches tall, and as straight as an arrow. The Kid had beautiful hazel eyes. Those eyes so quick and piercing were what saved his life many a time."
–Frank Coe
A rancher who also fought with Billy in the war.

"He weighed about 135 pounds, light complected [sic], with blue grey eyes and had very small hands and feet. His two front teeth were large and protruded. He was a nice and polite chap. One thing that struck me as very funny at the time was that he had on a black dress coat, his trouser legs stuffed in his boot tops and a large light hat."
–Dr. M.G. Paden
Lincoln County resident

"He was no better and no worse than the other boys of his age."
Mary Richards
The Kid's schoolteacher

"He was not handsome, but he had a certain sort of boyish good looks. He was always smiling and good-natured and very polite and danced remarkably well..."
–Paulita Maxwell
The Kid's sweetheart

"He had a beautiful voice and sang like a bird."
–George Coe

"He ate and laughed, drank and laughed, talked and laughed, fought and laughed, and killed and laughed."
–SHERIFF PAT GARRETT

THOSE WHO DIDN'T KNOW BILLY THE KID DESCRIBE HIM...

Johnny Mack Brown as Billy the Kid, (M-G-M, 1930)

"The Kid, in spite of his achievements, was a stripling, no larger than a woman, with black, straight hair and a cold, marble face that chilled the noonday sun."

–O. HENRY
The Caballero's Way, 1904

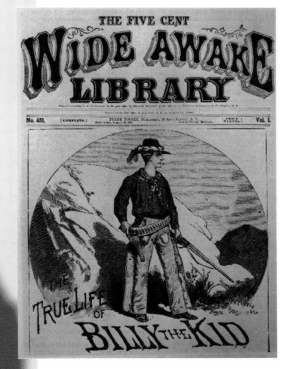

"The Kid wore a blue dragoon jacket of the finest broadcloth, heavily loaded down with gold embroidery, buckskin pants, dyed a jet black, with small tinkling bells sewed on the sides... drawers of the fines scarlet broadcloth... and a hat covered with gold and jewels..."

–EDMUND FABLE, JR.

"He was about five feet high, small hands and feet, dark, swarthy complection [sic], with hair as black as the ravens which infest those plains in great numbers. The distinguishing mark about the Kid were his eyes. They were black and very bright."

–J. E. SLIGH

FRONTIER FUNNIES?

It is labeled as "humor," but these examples from journals and newspapers of the day seem to prove nothing more than what seems "outrageous" and "sidesplitting" in one era is "irritatingly inappropriate" in another.

Would you be surprised to learn that the man who stole the judge's coat afterwards appeared in a law suit?

Fiery men are soon put out.

If you have a good wife, thank God every twenty minutes.

A little fire was not uncomfortable last night. Who wouldn't live in Santa Fe? – No heat, no flies no mosquitoes and but very little of the "root of evil."

A maiden lady down east lately advertised for a recipe to make secrets, as she had never yet had one that would bear keeping.

RURAL ADVANTAGES.

"IF THERE IS ONE THING MORE DELIGHTFUL THAN ANOTHER ABOUT LIVING IN THE COUNTRY, DEAR, IT IS THAT ONE IS ALWAYS CERTAIN TO GET SUCH SWEET, PURE, UNADULTERATED MILK."
"IT IS, INDEED, A COMFORT, ISN'T IT?"

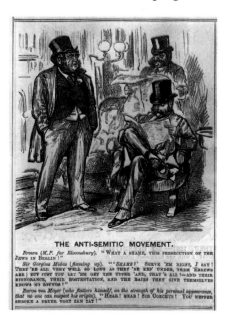

THE ANTI-SEMITIC MOVEMENT.
Brown (M.P. for Bloomsbury). "WHAT A SHAME, THIS PERSECUTION OF THE JEWS IN BERLIN!"
Sir Gorgius Midas (flaming up). "'SHAME!' SERVE 'EM RIGHT, I SAY! THEY 'RE ALL VERY WELL SO LONG AS THEY 'RE KEP' UNDER, THEM 'EBREWS ARE; BUT JUST YOU LET 'EM GET THE UPPER 'AND, THAT 'S ALL!—AND THEIR HIGNORANCE, THEIR HOSTENTATION, AND THE HAIRS THEY GIVE THEMSELVES KNOWS NO BOUNDS!"
Baron von Moses (who flatters himself, on the strength of his personal appearance, that no one can suspect his origin). "HEAR! HEAR! SIR GORGIUS! YOU NEVER SHOKEN A DRUER VORT ZAN ZAT!"

Confidential Friend (to elderly and not unattractive Spinster). "SO, DEAR, YOU 'VE GIVEN UP ADVOCATING WOMEN'S RIGHTS !"
Elderly Spinster. "YES, I NOW GO IN FOR WOMEN'S LEFTS."
Confidential Friend. "WOMEN'S LEFTS ! WHAT 'S THAT ?"
Elderly Spinster. "WIDOWERS, MY DEAR !"

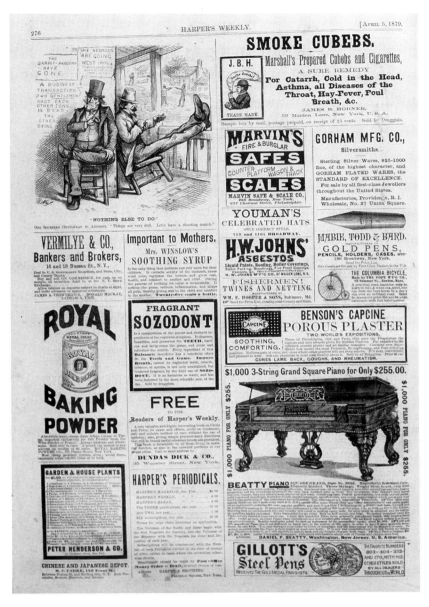

An example of the type of advertisements Billy saw in the press of the day. This page is from *Harper's Weekly*, 1879.

February 18, 1878
Tunstall killed.

February 21, 1878
The first telephone directory is issued, by the District Telephone Company of New Haven, Connecticut. It lists 50 names.

March 1, 1878
Constable J. B. Wilson appoints Richard Brewer special constable with Billy Bonney as deputy. Brewer forms a posse of about 15 men and they dub themselves the "Regulators."

March 6, 1878
Regulators, including the Kid, travel down the Pecos and capture Morton and Baker. The two men were directly involved in the death of Tunstall and they surrender on the condition they be taken to Lincoln for trial. Neither man makes it to Lincoln alive.

March 9, 1878
Jessie Evans is shot in the butt and Tom Hill is killed during the attempted robbery of a sheep camp near Tularosa.

March 10, 1878
Construction of a 12-foot high adobe wall around the McSween house continues. During a break, laborer Francisco Gomez helps Mrs. McSween "straighten a table leg."

Jimmy Dolan breaks his leg while jumping off a horse to "shoot at an unarmed man." Witnesses say he "fell off the wagon first."

March 11, 1878
Mr. McSween quits Lincoln for the safety of the Pecos. Mrs. McSween stays behind to "bone up" for a Spanish test.

WORSE CASE SCENARIO

April, 1878

Lincoln County is now in the unenviable position of having two opposing parties, both armed to the teeth, and both carrying legal authorization, roaming the countryside with warrants and weapons. Someone is bound to be in the wrong place at the wrong time, and his name is "Buckshot" Roberts.

The Gunfight at Blazer's Mill
April 4, 1878

McSween's men have named themselves the "Regulators." Each is bound by an oath – "The Iron Clad." It basically says they will fight to the death for each other. One of them is about to receive that "honor."

Coming over the mountains on the Rinconada trail, The Regulators drop into Blazer's Mill, which is on the road to Tularosa and La Mesilla. Riding in front is Richard Brewer, Tunstall's foreman and Captain of the Regulators. Behind him are George Coe, Frank Coe, Billy Bonney, John Middleton, Charlie Bowdre, Frank McNab, Doc Scurlock, Henry Brown and Fred Waite.

They rein in at 11 a.m. and herd their horses into the high walled corral. Brewer goes over to the main house and asks Mrs. Godfroy to fix them dinner.

Buckshot Roberts comes in from a mountain trail on the south. He is expecting a check in the mail and he wants to cash out and leave the country. He was a member of the posse that attacked Tunstall and he knows his name is on the Regulator's list.

Stopping short of the Mill, Roberts ties his packhorse to a tree and prods his mule across the creek to pick up his mail.

John Middleton, sitting outside the mess hall, spots Roberts and goes inside. Brewer says, "I have a warrant for Roberts."

Frank Coe, a neighbor of Roberts, goes outside to talk to him alone.

Unfortunately for Buckshot, he leaves his pistol belt on the saddle horn (respecting Dr. Blazer's gun rule). He carries his Winchester and runs into Coe who shakes his hand and takes him around the side of the house for a talk.

Impatiently, Brewer and his men wait to see if

Black on the Range

Frank Chisum, wrangler extraordinaire, is a good example of the "colored" cowboys who worked the ranges of New Mexico during Billy the Kid's time. Benjamin Franklin Daley was his real name, and he was bought by John Chisum in Fort Worth, Texas, for $400. Chisum then set Frank free with the offer to work for the Jinglebob. By "work" Chisum meant that he would provide room and board but no pay. Before he died, Chisum settled with Frank, giving him several hundred head of cattle (Chisum never spent money when he could spend cattle). Frank was a dead shot and acted as Chisum's bodyguard. When Chisum came down with smallpox, Frank rode 150 miles nonstop to get medicine for his friend.

Frank can persuade Roberts to surrender.

"We talked for half and hour," Coe said. "I begged him to surrender, but the answer was no, no, no. I think he was the bravest man I ever met—not a bit excited, knowing too that his life was in his hands."

Brewer finally gets tired of waiting and three volunteers stomp around the corner of the house to end the stalemate.

Charlie Bowdre is in front, followed by John Middleton and George Coe. Charlie pulls his hog leg and demands,"Roberts, throw up your hands."

Buckshot stands and brings his Winchester up to his hip (he has a shoulder injury which earned him his nickname).

Roberts replies, "Not much, Mary Ann."

Bowdre and Roberts fire at the same time. Roberts' bullet hits Bowdre's belt buckle which drops his gunbelt to the ground. The bullet then ricochets down the gunbarrel of George Coe's gun and takes off his trigger finger.

Bowdre's bullet hits Robert's just below the belly. "The dust flew from his clothes from both sides," says Frank Coe, who leaps out of the hornets nest.

Roberts staggers backwards, firing as he goes. His next bullet nails Middleton in the chest. Another hits the barrel of Doc Scurlock's holstered pistol and courses down his leg. The Kid is "shaved" in the arm and backs out as "it was too hot there for him."

"I never saw a man that could handle a Winchester as fast as he could," marveled Frank Coe later.

Roberts stumbles into Blazer's office, rips a mattress off a bed and throws it in the doorway as a breastwork. He pulls a Springfield rifle off the wall (his Winchester is empty) and takes up a position on the mattress.

With wounded men sprawled all around him, Brewer, vows to "have that man out" if he "has to pull the house down."

He sprints down to a footbridge, crosses the creek and takes up a position about 125 yards from the house. Peeking up from behind a pile of logs Brewer fires at Roberts. The bullet smashes harmlessly into the wall behind Buckshot's head. Roberts, mortally wounded, takes note of the puff of smoke from Brewer's gun and takes aim with the Springfield. Brewer peeks up once again to see how his shot did. As he does, Buckshot let loose with the big Springfield. The bullet hits Brewer in the left eye, leaving a tiny blue mark, then blows out the back of his skull.

The Regulators, in disarray, leave the battlefield and their leader behind.

September 17, 1991
Art Blazer, great-grandson of Dr. Blazer says, "nobody in the family could hit a damn thing with that rifle."

A MAP OF THE LINCOLN COUNTY WAR

White Oaks

Ft. Stanton

Lincoln

Brewer's Farm

San Patricio

Roswell

Blazer's Mill

Chisum' Ranch

Tularosa

White Sands

Tunstall's Ranch

Paul's Ranch

San Augustine Pass

Shedd's Ranch

Seven Rivers

Las Cruces

La Mesilla

At the time of the war, Lincoln County encompassed more than 28,000 square miles. The distances they travelled by horseback in a given day are almost inconceivable today. For example, Tunstall took off from Lincoln and rode to Chisum's Ranch a distance of more than 60 miles. The next morning, he rode to his ranch on the Feliz, another 50 miles. After several hours of sleep he joined his cowboys on their ill-fated jaunt to Lincoln, a distance of 50 more miles!

A QUERIDA IN EVERY PLAZA

**Abrano Garcia
Fort Sumner**

**Fredricke Deolavera
Anton Chico**

*"He had more sweethearts
on the creek than a little."*
–ADD CASEY

*"Billy the Kid, I may tell you,
fascinated many women. His
record as a heart-breaker was
quite as formidable, you might
say, as his record as a man-
killer… in every placita in the
Pecos some little señorita was
proud to be known as
his querida."*
–PAULITA MAXWELL

**Lily Huntress
Roswell**

**Miquilita Carrera
Puerto de Luna**

**Emily Schulander
Las Vegas**

PECOS PRINCESS

Sallie Chisum, the prettiest girl on the Pecos, describes meeting Billy the Kid:

"...I remember how frightened I was the first time he came. I was sitting in the living room when word was brought that this famous desperado had arrived. I fell into a panic. I pictured him in all the evil ugliness of a bloodthirsty ogre. I half-expected he would slit my throat if he didn't like my looks.

"'Howdy, Miss Chisum, I'm pleased to meet you,' he said with a deferential bow in the phrase that was *de rigueur* on the frontier.

"'You're Billy the Kid?' I gasped.

"'That's what they call me,' he drawled in a soft voice.

"I sank down on the sofa and laughed until the tears came. He must have thought I was crazy but he laughed, too.

"' Well,' I said when I was able to speak, 'of course I owe you an explanation and an apology. But, you see, I – I didn't expect to find you looking like you do.'

"'Yes,' he answered good-naturedly, 'I understand.'

"And we both fell laughing again."

"As far as dress was concerned, he always looked as if he had just stepped out of a band-box. In broad-brimmed white hat, dark coat and vest, gray trousers worn over his boots, a gray flannel shirt and black four-in-the-hand tie, and sometimes-would you believe it?– a flower in his lapel, he was a dashing figure and quite the dandy.

"Many a gallop across country Billy the Kid and I took together, and many a pleasant evening we sat talking for hours on the front gallery."

"My heart was in my mouth as I heard his step on the porch and knew that Uncle John was bringing him in. In a daze I heard Uncle John saying with a wave of his hand, 'Sallie, this is my friend, Billy the Kid.' A good-looking, clear-eyed boy stood there with his hat in his hand, smiling at me."

–SALLIE CHISUM

WOMEN'S WORK IS NEVER FUN

While the men are out shooting at each other, the women folk are safe and snug at home. Not quite.

Ma'am Jones of the Pecos has ten kids – nine of them boys. She lives 150 miles from the nearest doctor and her husband is gone freighting goods to and from their store, nine days out of ten.

Her son Sammy falls into some broken glass and comes in the house with his eye-lid hanging by a thread. She takes a needle and thread and *sews his eyelid back on!*

Meanwhile, the women of New Mexico have to deal with the following fun:

June, 1877

A grasshopper plague wipes out crops in the Rio Arriba area. Farmers try sprinkling ashes on the plants and using lime water, but neither works. The grasshoppers come in through the windows and doors covering furniture and food. There is no relief for months.

July, 1877

The black smallpox plague rips through southeastern New Mexico territory killing three Mescalaro Apache chiefs in addition to hundreds of men, women and especially children. Chisum gets it. So does Richard Brewer, Rob Widenman John Tunstall, Robert Ollinger and Lily Casey.

Lily describes what happened in her home on the Hondo:

"[My mother] was compelled to make several trips to Lincoln. When she returned from one with headache and a pain in her chest we were alarmed. That night she went to bed early and asked me to bring her some coal oil (kerosene) which she used extensively for

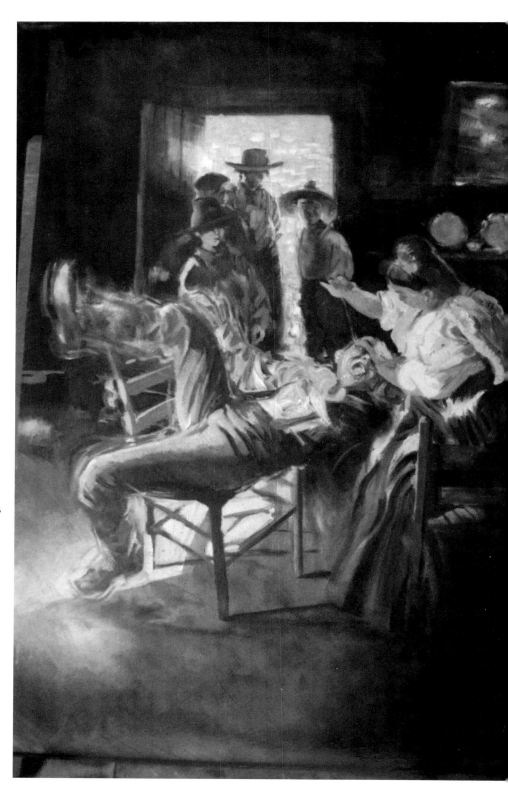

"The only kind of equality that counts is being equal to the occasion."

An advertisement, published in *Tales, Sketches, Poetry and Music*, 1872.

SEWING MACHINES.

A HOUSEHOLD SONG.

Air—"AULD LANG SYNE."

In all the range of household art,
    There's nothing can compare
With a WHEELER & WILSON Sewing Machine,
    For driving away dull care.
            For driving away, etc.

Turn with your foot its rapid wheel,
    Spool off your thread with a whirl,
Stitch with its sharp stiletto of steel—
    You've a garment for boy or girl.
            You've a garment, etc.

And what used to be but a day of toil,
    Is now but an hour of play,
As you rapidly finish your dainty work
    And lay it, completed, away.
            And lay it, etc.

Oh! a fairy bright is the Sewing Machine,
    With its braider and corder complete,
And a neater Christmas Gift, I ween,
    You'll not find on Montgomery street.
            You'll not find, etc.

various illnesses. She rubbed it on her skin, including her scalp, then told me to give the children their supper and put them to bed.

"The next morning Mother's body was covered with pustules. We learned that the use of Kerosene had been a mistake, for her scalp became a solid scab. To treat the skin it was necessary to cut her long black hair as close as possible. Her breasts were a solid blister as were her hands and arms, and her body swelled to twice its normal size and turned black. For twenty-five days she lay in bed, attended by myself and successive neighbor women.

"…Because we were working day and night not only with Mother but others who were ill, mice invaded the house. We had no time to attempt to eradicate them and they ran over the floors and even on the beds. When mother was suffering terribly from her hands and arms she raised them above her head, and the pustules were bitten by mice. Perhaps she was delirious; at least she did not call us, and she said that the opening of the pustules afforded great relief."

Thanks for sharing!

THE BIG KILLING

April 23, 1878

J. J. Dolan & Co. "temporarily" suspends business. A mass meeting of citizens passes a resolution "requesting" members of the "Irish firm" to leave Lincoln.

May 10, 1878

L. G. Murphy leaves Lincoln for a sanitarium in Santa Fe. He is accompanied by Jimmy Dolan and will never return. Murphy suffers severe delirium tremens and dies October 20.

May 19, 1878

Manuel Segovia, alias "The Indian," is killed by a group of Regulators near Seven Rivers. He was in the posse that killed Tunstall.

June 18, 1878

Congress passes the Posse Comitatus Act which forbids military intervention in civil disturbances.

"The Kid was lively and McSween was sad. McSween sat with his head down, and the Kid shook him and told him to get up, that they were going to make a break."

– SUSAN MCSWEEN

July 14, 1878

Tired of running, McSween and forty of his men reach Lincoln. As the small army comes thundering in, Francisco Gomez is spotted fixing a window in the rear of the McSween house in his underwear. The McSween faction takes up strategic positions around the town, including the Tunstall store, the Montaño store and the Ellis store. George Coe lodges himself in the grain storage shed behind the Tunstall store, which commands a view of McSween's back yard.

July 15, 1878

A large Dolan party arrives from the west and begins firing at the McSween house. Citizens appeal to Col. Dudley at Fort Stanton to come and intercede. He tells them his hands are tied by the Posse Comitatus Act.

July 16, 1878

Intermittent firing all day. Mary Ealy, later recalled, "The shooting, yelling and screaming were distressing." Dolan, who is still smarting from his broken leg, makes his headquarters at the Wortley hotel. He is joined there by Jesse Evans, Bob and Wallace Olinger, John Kinney, the Jones boys and others. Dolan's men ask Col. Dudley for a howitzer. Sheriff Peppin huddles with Dolan and they decide to delegate – they send Jack Long with instructions to serve the warrants on McSween. Mr. Long marches right up to the front door and demands the surrender of the wanted men. Someone inside yells that they too have warrants.

"Where?" Demands Long.

The Voice booms "In the barrels of our guns!" as the McSween men cut loose with a volley of rifle fire that sends Long flying over the picket fence to safety.

Private Berry Robinson is bringing Dudley's reply on the

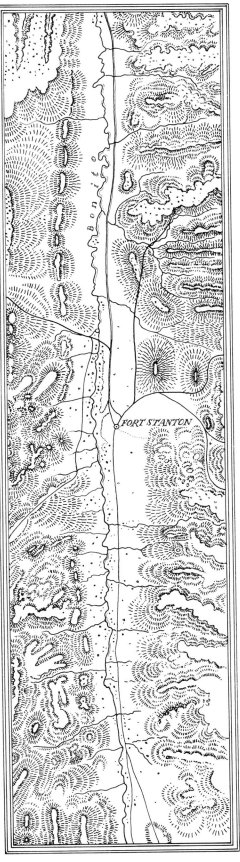

howitzer request, when he is fired upon from the plaza. Both factions blame each other but this provides Dudley with an excuse to intercede.

July 19, 1878

Around noon, Col. Dudley arrives in Lincoln with four officers, one company of cavalry and one company of infantry, for a total of 35 men. He also has a brass twelve-pounder and a Gatling gun with 2,000 rounds of ammunition. His stated mission is to "place soldiers in the town of Lincoln for the preservation of the lives of the women and children."

In the midst of all this madness, the mailman comes through and

McSween orders three dollars worth of stamps and the Kid sends a love note to Sallie Chisum. Joseph Smith writes to his former boss in Roswell. He closes with: "[The Murphys] tried to scare us out but we didn't scare worth a damn. Well, I must quit writing. Good luck to you. Tell Bill Nagle he can have them gloves."

Dudley camps on the east side of town across from the Montaño store and declares his neutrality. In the same breath, he orders the howitzer pointed at the Montaño store. As the gun crew shouts their cadences, all the McSween men inside the store flee. And all the McSween men inside the Patrón store flee. Dolan's men take advantage of the situation and charge the Ellis store. Bowdre, Middleton, Scurlock and the men stationed there flee also. In one "neutral," move, Col. Dudley has tipped the scales totally against Alexander McSween.

Susan McSween does not take this lying down. She comes storming out of her house, and marches down to confront Dudley. As she walks, several snipers take pot shots at her, the bullets ripping the ground at her feet. She keeps on going, petticoats flying and her head up.

Susan demands to know why Dudley is allowing Dolan's men to fire on her house which has women and children inside.

Dudley tells her the women have no business being in there and adds, "I cannot give you protection while you allow such men as Billy Kid, Jim French, and others of like character to be in your house."

The conversation goes downhill from there and ends with Dudley casting aspersions on her moral character. "The ladies I associate

"I'm not afraid to die like a man fighting but I would not like to be killed like a dog unarmed."

– BILLY THE KID

BAD BOY, GOOD COPY

"BILLY THE KID," AS A COW-BOY.

During the last 110 years or so, the press has had a field day with Billy the Kid. As the times change so does Billy – at least on paper.

"he was a low down vulgar cut-throat, with probably not one redeeming quality."
– *Grant County Herald*, July 28, 1881

"How many men he killed, how many cattle he stole, how many deeds of daring deviltry and cruelty he perpetrated will probably never be known until the record books of damnation are opened, and cowboys and Congressmen, law-makers and law-breakers, presidents, pirates, governors and thugs are summoned to judgement."
– *Grant County Herald*, August 20, 1881

"A genius for depopulation... a Robin Hood for the mesas, a Don Juan of New Mexico whose youthful daring has never been equalled in our entire frontier history."
– Bookmarker for *The Saga of Billy the Kid*
by Walter Noble Burns, 1926

"Actually Billy the Kid was just a little, small-sized cow- and horse-thief who lived grubbily and missed legal hanging by only a few days. He killed, or took part in killing, several people; but his killings were more often on the order of safe butchery than stand-up-and-fight-it-out gun battles."
– *Pardner of the Wind*
by Jack Thorpe

"The Kid is now viewed as a victim of circumstances who deserved a better life."
– *The Western Hero in History and Legend*
by Kent Ladd Steckmesser, 1965

with don't use such language," the Colonel sniffs. (The "language" Susan used is "too thin," as in, "Your being in town with your troops today looks a little too thin to me." Bad girl.)

Around mid-afternoon, Dolan's men try a different tactic. After one unsuccessful attempt, they manage to set fire to the wood-frame lean-to on the northwest corner of McSween's house. The men who started it don't get away clean though. George Coe, stationed in Tunstall's grain shed spots them as they retreat and fires on them. The two Dolan men jump into an open privy. The firestarters are trapped there all day and when things get boring, Coe peppers the outhouse with bullets, keeping the duo up to their necks in... shinola.

The fire burns slowly but inexorably and the occupants move back room by room. As the flames pick up so does the firing. Military officers estimate more than two thousand rounds are fired during the late afternoon. Finally, the women and children are evacuated.

Dolan's men move in for the kill. At dusk, a group led by Billy the Kid makes a run for it. A young law student, Harvey Morris, is shot dead as he runs beside Billy. The Kid and several others make it to the brush along the river and escape into the hills. McSween is in a second group and he is not so lucky. Trapped in the back yard he and four others are shot down next to the chicken house at point blank range.

In the morning, Susan and her sister approach her smoldering house. She finds her husband and says, "Somebody please find me a canvas, the chickens are pecking my husband's eyes out."

ONE LOUSY PHOTO

An ongoing photo analysis of the only "known" photograph of Billy the Kid has revealed some tantalizing clues. "It's like looking at enraged mud turtles," says Grant Romer, of the Lincoln County Heritage Trust Photo Project.
The findings so far:

On his head is an inexpensive slouch hat with a side crease.

His sweater appears to have a hood.

The photographer used and Anthony four-tube camera with a six second exposure. Billy probably paid 25 cents for four images.

Behind Billy's right foot can be seen a leg of a stand used for stability during long exposures.

His teeth appear to confirm what a contemporary said about him, "he could eat pumpkins through a picket fence."

A hand of the photo assistant can be seen holding the light reflector.

Photo experts think the design on Billy's bib shirt is a nautical anchor.

His sweater is at least two sizes too large.

Billy wears a gambler's pinky ring.

He carries an 1873 Winchester

While developing the wet plate, the photographer handled the bottom corners leaving his thumbprints. Four exposures were on the ferreotype and the image was reversed as shown, right. This led to the erroneous assumption that Billy the Kid was left-handed.

'YOU CAN'T SCARE ME BOYS, I KNOW IT'S YOU'

Huston Chapman

February 18, 1879

It is one year to the day that John Tunstall was murdered.

McSween is dead. The bodies have stopped piling up and the embers seem to have died down. There is a new Governor in Santa Fe. His name is Lew Wallace and he is an ex-Civil War general turned attorney. He figures the appointment to a far off territory like New Mexico will give him plenty of time to work on his second novel.

In Lincoln, the evening starts off on an odd note: Jimmy Dolan runs into lawyer Huston Chapman of Las Vegas, who has been hired by Susan McSween to make a case against Col. Dudley. Of all places, Dolan says, "I met him on the evening of the occurrence after dark on his arrival entering the house of Mrs. McSween, where a party of citizens were assembled. Mrs. McSween giving a Musical entertainment. Salutations passed between us, he expressing himself as being pleased with the proceedings of the afternoon. I [replied] in

Only in a small town! Jimmy Dolan (third from left) runs into Huston Chapman (rubbing jaw, second from left) at a piano recital given by Susan McSween.

"The first thing we do, let's kill all the lawyers."

–SHAKESPEARE

like manner, after which we parted, he retiring to his room. This was the last time I saw Mr. Chapman."

Eye-witnesses disagree with Mr. Dolan.

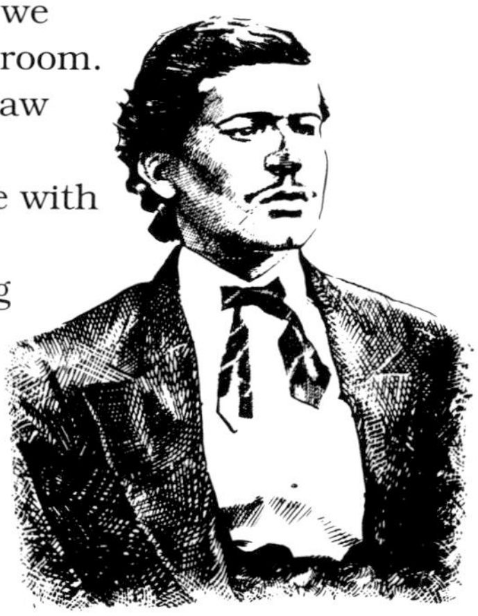

Juan Patrón

Tired of all the running and fighting, Billy the Kid has sent a note to Jesse Evans proposing a parley.

Jesse agrees and the two Bravos meet in Lincoln. In Evans' party are Billy Campbell and Jimmy Dolan. Among the Kid's party are Tom O'Folliard and Doc Scurlock.

The two sides meet on either side of facing adobe walls. Evans opens the ball by saying he ought to kill Billy.

"I don't care to open negotiations with a fight," the Kid shouts, "but if you'll come at me three at a time, I'll whip the whole damned bunch of you!"

Eventually the two parties warily approach each other in the street and the Kid and Evans shake.

To celebrate, they repair to a saloon and draw up a peace treaty. They agree on, among other things, that neither party will kill any member of the other party without giving notice (this is not a joke – they *really* agreed on this.)

By ten o'clock they are rip-roaring drunk. Spilling out onto the street, the boisterous boys show up at Juan Patrón's house. Billy Campbell tries to shoot him. Fortunately for Juan, someone knocks Campbell's gun hand away at the last second.

Unfortunately for Huston Chapman, the sloshed celebrants encounter him seeking a poultace for an aching tooth. After a brief exchange, Chapman is shot dead.

The killing reverberates across the territory. Fears of more warfare reach the Palace of Governors in Santa Fe. Lew Wallace will have to put his novel aside and travel to Lincoln. He is not amused.

The Chapman Murder

Huston Chapman lost his left arm as a boy in a hunting accident. On the night of February 18 he has just arrived from Las Vegas and a very sore tooth brings him out on the street to seek a poultace for his face.

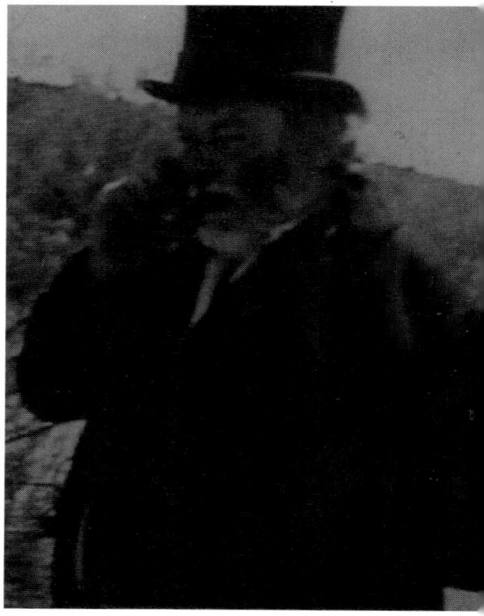

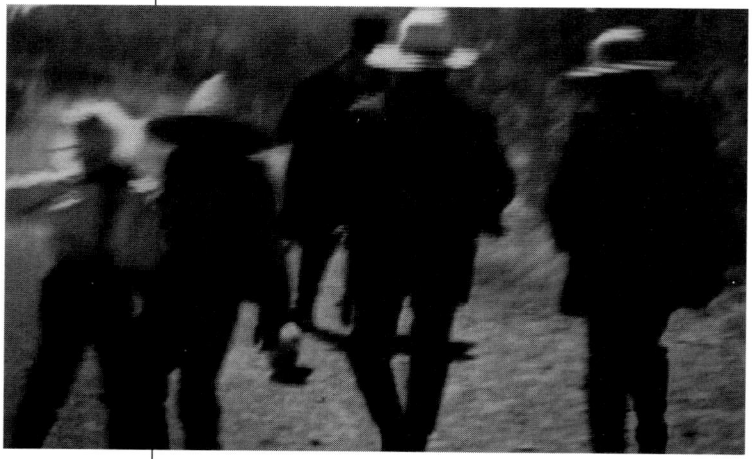

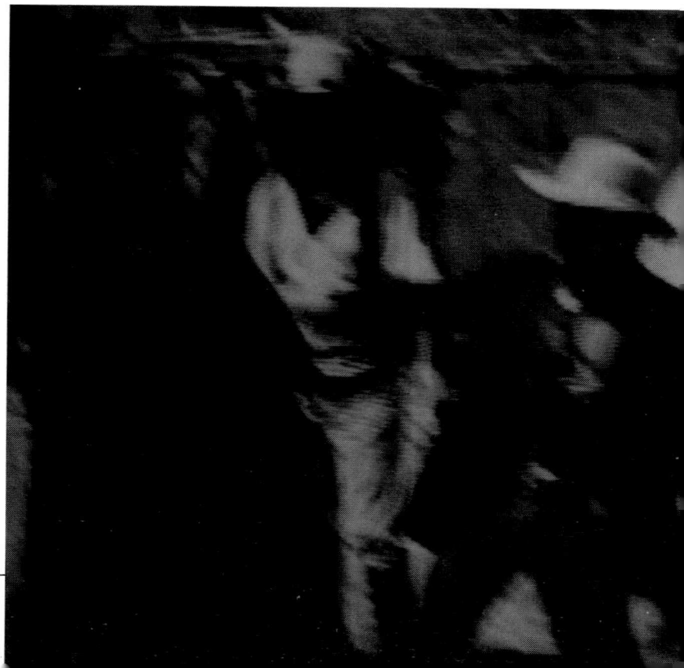

He encounters the mob and Campbell blocks his path, demanding that Chapman dance. Chapman shakes his head. "I don't propose to dance for a drunken mob." Then he adds, "You can't scare me boys, I know it's you, and it's no use. You've tried that before. Am I talking to Mr. Dolan?" "No," Jesse Evans says, "but you're talking to a damned good friend of his." At This moment, Jimmy Dolan fires his rifle into the ground, and Campbell reacts, pulling the trigger on his revolver. Chapman gasps, "My God, I am killed!" He collapses, his clothes set afire from the powder flash. The Kid tries to run but Dolan grabs him by the nape of the neck. Later, having more drinks and oysters up the street at McCullum's, one of the party ventures that a weapon should be planted on the corpse. The Kid volunteers. He leaves the bar and skins out. Lincoln wakes up to another man for breakfast.

THE KID MEETS THE GOVERNOR

W. H. Bonney,

Come to the house of old Squire Wilson (not the lawyer) at nine (9) o'clock next Monday night alone. I don't mean his office, but his residence. Following along the foot of the mountains south of the town, come in on that side, and knock at the east door. I have authority to exempt you from prosecution if you will testify to what you say you know.

Lew Wallace

"Billy the Kid kept the appointment punctually," Wallace related.

"At the time designated, I heard a knock on the door, and called out, 'Come in.' The door opened slowly and carefully, and there stood the young fellow generally known as the Kid, his Winchester in his right hand, his revolver in his left.

"'I was sent for to meet the governor here at 9 o'clock,' said the Kid. 'Is he here?' I rose to my feet, saying, 'I am Governor Wallace,' and held out my hand. When we had shaken hands, I invited the young fellow to be seated so that we may talk together... When he had taken his seat I proceeded to unfold the plan I had in mind to enable him to testify to what he knew about the killing of Chapman... I closed with a promise, 'In return for your doing this I will let you go scot free with a pardon in your pocket for all your misdeeds.'"

Days after, The Kid submits to a phony arrest and is kept at Casa de Patrón where the Governor witnesses the scene on the following page.

☞

"A precious specimen named 'The Kid,' whom the sheriff is holding here in the Plaza, as it is called, is an object of tender regard. I heard singing and music the other night; going to the door, I found the minstrels of the village actually serenading the fellow in his prison."

—GOVERNOR LEW WALLACE

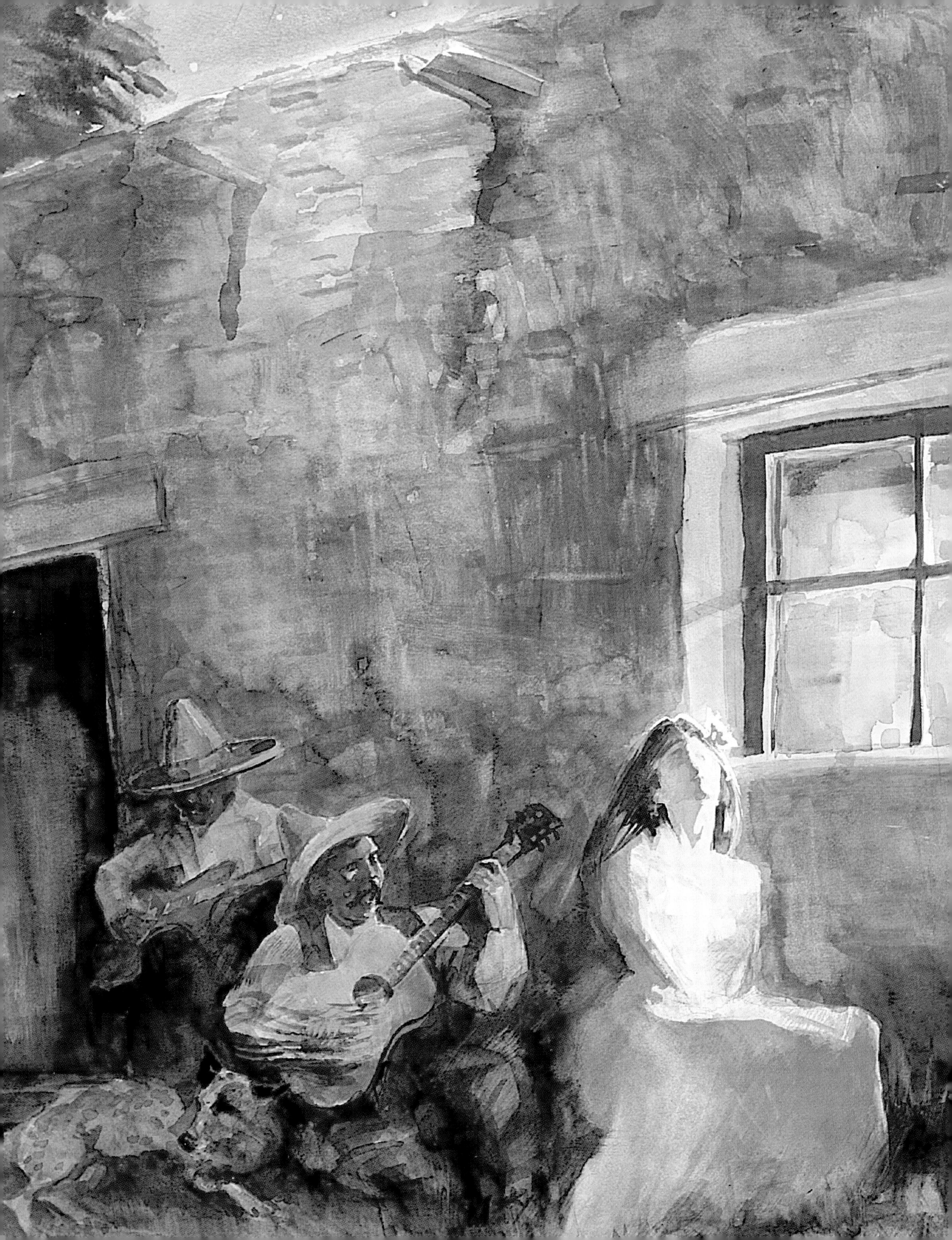

PLEADING HIS CASE

December 12, 1880

After walking most of the way back to Fort Sumner in the snow, Billy sits down to write Governor Wallace. In his letter he attempts to vindicate his growing image as the boy "captain of a band of outlaws."

Gov Lew Wallace
Dear Sir

I noticed in the Las Vegas GAZETTE a piece which stated that Billy "the" Kid, the name by which I am known in the country was the captain of a band of outlaws who hold forth at the Portales. There is no such organization in existence. So the gentleman must have drawn very heavily on the imagination. My business at the White Oaks at the time I was waylaid and my horse killed was to see Judge Leonard who had my case in hand. He had written to me to come up, that he thought he could get everything straightened up I did not find him at the Oaks & should have gone to Lincoln if I had met with no accident. After mine and Billie Wilsons horses were killed we both made our way to a station, forty miles from the Oaks kept by Mr. Greathouse. When I got up next morning the house was surrounded by an outfit led by one Carlyle, who came into the house and demanded a surrender. I asked for their papers and they had none. So I concluded it amounted to nothing more than a mob and told Carlyle that he would have to stay in the house and lead the way out that night. Soon after a note was brought in stating that if Carlyle did not come out inside of five minutes they would kill the station keeper (Greathouse) who had left the house and was with them. In a short time a shot was fired on the outside and Carlyle thinking Greathouse was killed jumped through the window breaking the sash as he went and was killed by his own Party they think it was me trying to make my escape. The Party withdrew.

I have been at Sumner since I left Lincoln making my living gambling... J.S. Chisum is the man who got me into trouble and was benefited Thousands by it and is now doing all he can against me. There is no Doubt but what there is a great deal of stealing going on in the Territory and a great deal of property is taken across the Plains as it is a good outlet but so far as my being at the head of a band there is nothing of it in several instances I have recovered stolen property when there was no chance to get an officer to do it.

One instance for Hugh Zuber post office Puerto de Luna another for Pablo Analla same place.

If some impartial party were to investigate this matter they would find it far different from the impression put out by Chisum and his tools.

Yours Respect.
W. H. Bonney

The day after Billy wrote his letter, Governor Wallace offered this reward posted in a Santa Fe newspaper.

SQUAD BUSTER

November, 1880

John Chisum puts up Patrick Floyd Garrett's name for sheriff of Lincoln County. Specifically, Chisum wants Garrett to clean out "that squad east of Sumner." Before he's elect-ed, Garrett meets with Bowdre and several of the gang and tells them to clear out like the Coes did and come back when things die down. Bowdre thinks about it but Billy turns it down flat.

Patrick F. Garrett

November 27, 1880

Billy and his gang are sur-rounded at the Greathouse ranch north of White Oaks. Jim Carlyle, a member of the posse is killed. Billy escapes.

December 13, 1880

Garrett and his brother-in-law, Barney Mason, join forces with the Texas cowboys sent over by the Canadian River cattle owners. A massive snowstorm blankets the Pecos country. Garrett and his posse ride night and day to reach Fort Sumner.

December 19, 1880

Waiting at Manuela Bowdre's house in Fort Sumner, a lookout spots five riders coming out of a powder-blue fog. Garrett grabs his rifle and says, "No one but the men we want are riding this time of night."

"OH, MY GOD, IS IT POSSIBLE THAT I MUST DIE?"

Tom O'Folliard

Pat Garrett continues his version of events:

"I was under the porch and close against the wall, partly hidden by some harness hanging there. Chambers was close behind him. I whispered, 'That's him.' They rode on up until O'Folliard's horse's head was under the porch. When I called 'Halt!' O'Folliard reached for his pistol, but before he could draw it, Chambers and I both fired. His horse wheeled and ran at least a hundred and fifty yards. As quick as possible I fired at Pickett, but the flash of Chambers' gun disconcerted my aim, and I missed him. But one might have thought by the way he ran and yelled that I had a dozen bullets in him. When O'Folliard's horse ran with him, he was uttering cries of mortal agony and we were convinced that he had

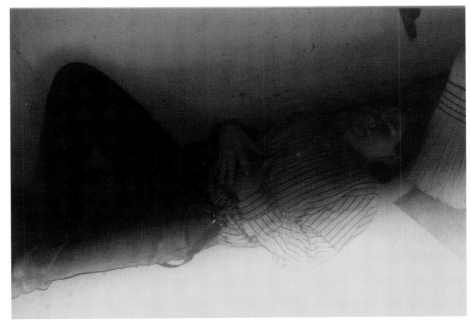

received a death wound. But he wheeled his horse, and as he rode slowly back, said, "Don't shoot, Garrett, I am killed."

Mason, from the other side of the house where he had been stationed, called out, "Take your medicine, old boy; take your medicine," and was going to O'Folliard's assistance. But fearing that it might be a feint and that O'Folliard might attempt revenge on Mason, I called out a warning to the latter to be careful how he approached the wounded man.

Holding our guns down on him, we went up to him, took his gun out of the scabbard, lifted him off his horse, carried him into the house, and laid him down. Then taking off his pistol, which was full-cocked, we examined him and found that he was shot through the left side just below the heart, his coat having been cut across the front by a bullet.

Mason again told him to take his medicine. O'Folliard replied, "It's the best medicine I ever took."

Once he exclaimed, "Oh, my God, is it possible that I must die?"

I said to him just before he died, "Tom, your time is short." He answered, "The sooner the

better; I will be out of pain then."
He blamed no one and told us
who had been in the Kid's party
with him."

While O'Folliard is dying several
of the men go back to their card
game on the blanket.

The next day, the posse buries
the outlaw and waits. Garrett
receives word of the gang's whereabouts and on the evening of
December 21, thirteen riders
make tracks towards Stinking
Springs.

YOUNG LAWMEN

Garrett's possemen were not
experienced gunmen or lawmen.
In fact they were not much more
than boys. As posse member
James East put it, "Late in the fall
of 1880, cattlemen [in the Texas
panhandle] lost a good many cattle by their drifting across on the
plains and Billy the Kid gathering
them up and took them to Fort
Sumner.

Moore [East's boss] sent us over
to kill or capture the Kid, who was
stealing the cattle. The reason he
sent me and some other fellows
was to get us off the ranch as we
weren't helping him steal. He
didn't care whether we got killed
or not. We left the ranch
November 16, 1880.

After spending about a month in
Anton Chico drinking, gambling
and whoring they met up with
Garrett who offered to split the
reward if they could bring Billy in.

It's interesting to note that
Garrett couldn't get anybody in
New Mexico to go after the Kid.
Everyone, up and down the Pecos,
either feared him or loved him.

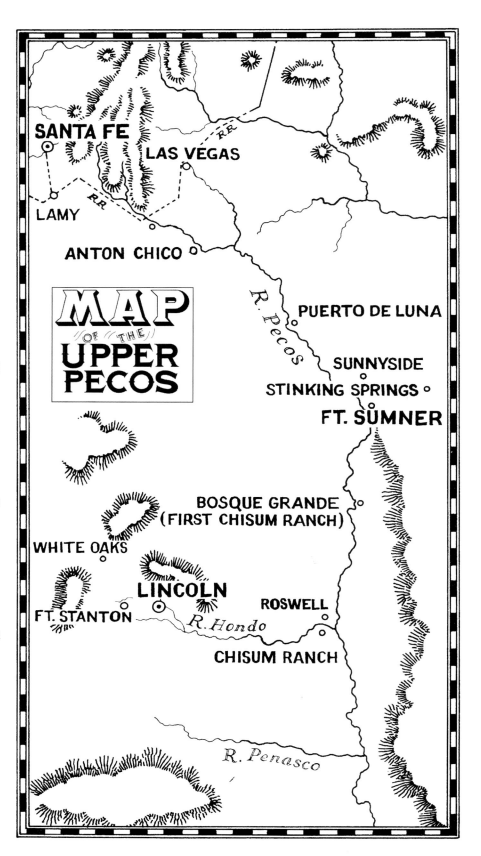

STINKING BADGES

December 21, 1880

In the midnight light of the snow, Garrett has no trouble tracking the outlaws to an abandoned rock house on Arroyo Taiban. It is called Stinking Springs. Garrett divides his party into two groups and suggests they rush the house in the darkness and take the Kid. Stewart, of the Canadian cowboys, declines. So they wait out the cold night on their blankets. Several of the boys crawl up to the walls of the house. They can hear loud snoring inside. Three horses are tied to the vigas outside. Two of the horses are inside with the outlaws.

Only Garrett and Mason know what the Kid looks like. It is agreed they will shoot the Kid on sight rather than risk a protracted fight. Garrett has learned that the Kid was last seen wearing a Chihuahua sombrero with an Irish green hatband. If he sees Billy, he will raise his hand as a signal and they will all shoot.

The hours crawl by. Several men suffer frostbite on their toes.

"In the darkness, Death crouched, waiting."

Finally, the first frigid light cracks the eastern horizon. Garrett and his men hear stirring inside the rock house. The horses tied outside begin to snort and pace. Seven Winchesters cover the door. Out steps a lone figure carrying a nosebag for the horses. He is wearing a wide-brimmed hat with a green hatband. Garrett gives the signal and seven thumb-sized projectiles, travelling 800 feet -per- second, rip into the twilight.

'I WISH, I WISH...'

Garrett recounts what happened next:

"Our victim was Charlie Bowdre. He turned and reeled back into the house. In a moment Wilson called to me from the house and said that Bowdre was killed and wanted to come out. I told him to come out with his hands up. As he started, the Kid caught hold of his belt, drew his revolver around in front of him and said, 'They have murdered you, Charlie, but you can get revenge. Kill some of the sons of bitches before you die.' ...he came straight to me, motioning towards the house and almost strangling with blood, said, 'I wish– I wish– I wish–' then in a whisper, 'I am dying!' I took hold of him, laid him gently on my blankets, and he died almost immediately."

He probably wishes he hadn't worn that hat.

The case of the bizarre twin photos; at first glance it seems obvious that the photos of Charlie and Manuella Bowdre on these two pages were taken at the same sitting. But take a closer look. How and why is his holster flopped in the two photos? Possible explanation: he is wearing *two* guns. And at the suggestion of the photographer, Charlie has moved his right holster around back and pulled his left holster around into a cross-draw position.

This photo was taken off of Charlie's body by Pat Garrett at Stinking Springs (note the blood stains).

EAST OUT WEST

December 25, 1880

James East is in the posse that captured the Kid, Rudabaugh, Pickett and Wilson. Garrett wants to make a dash for Vegas in the snow before any of Billy's friends in the area get wise. East explains what happened next: "We got a cold snack at the store and struck straight out for Las Vegas with the prisoners. We rode night and day to get there as we wanted to get them turned over to the government. We started after 12 o'clock, rode all afternoon and all night, and got to Puerto de Luna in the morning. The snow was still on the ground and it was hard to travel. Wilcox had furnished a wagon and had provisions in it. We got something to eat. I was put on guard by myself with a long adobe room and a fireplace in one end and a door in the other. We had Rudabaugh and Kid chained together. The others were not chained. They put me in there and locked us all in. I sat down on a pile of wood by the door and the prisoners were in the other end.

After we sat there awhile, Billy said, "Jim, do you have anything

to smoke?"

I said, "Yes, I have some tobacco."

He said he had some papers.

I said, "Billy, I'll throw you the tobacco."

He said, "No, I'll come and get it," and he and Dave started across the room toward me.

I said, "Hold on, Billy! If you come any farther, I'm going to shoot you."

They started on and I said, "Hold on, Billy, if you make another step, I'll shoot you."

He stopped and said, "You're the most suspicious damn man I ever saw." He turned back and I pitched him my tobacco. He threw it back and said he didn't want any of my tobacco.

The boys were gone about an hour to get dinner. I was locked in and Pat had the key in his pocket, and that was a mighty foolish thing to do. He got two of his deputies killed in somewhat the same way."

ZERO BLANKETS

James East tells about travelling on horseback as they trailed the Kid: "We had a blanket apiece. I got snowblindness as we crossed Piedranal Plains about 40 miles of level snow covered the country. It was below zero. We slept out every night but two. Tom froze his feet. He would dig down in the snow and go to sleep. When the snow warmed it would be warm. The snow storm came and froze one of Tom's feet, and froze my face so that my eyelashes came out."

A New Suit for Billy

Garrett arrives in Las Vegas with his prisoners on December 26, 1880. He and his posse are instant celebrities. Everyone wants to buy them a drink. They oblige.

A *Las Vegas Gazette* reporter is admitted to the jail the next morning. He files this report:

Mike Cosgrove, the obliging male contractor, who often met the boys while on business down on the Pecos, had just gone in with five large bundles. The doors at the entrance stood open and a large crowd strained their necks to get a glimpse of the prisoners, who stood in the passageway like children waiting for a Christmas tree distribution. One by one the bundles were unpacked, disclosing a good suit for each man. Mr. Cosgrove remarked that he wanted "to see the boys go away in style."

"...You appear to take it easy,"the reporter said.

"Yes! What's the use of looking on the gloomy side of everything. The laugh's on me this time," Billy said. The looking about the placita, he asked "is the jail at Santa Fe any better than this?"

...He was the attraction of the show, as he stood there, lightly kicking the toes of his boots on the stone pavement to keep his feet warm, one would scarcely mistrust that he was the hero of the "Forty Thieves" romance which this paper has been running in serial form for six weeks or more.

He did look human, indeed, but there was nothing very mannish about him in appearance, for he looked and acted a mere boy. He is about five feet eight or nine inches tall, slightly built and lithe weighing about 140; a frank open countenance, looking like a schoolboy, with the traditional silky fuzz on his upper lip; clear blue eyes, with a rougish snap about them; light hair and complexion. He is, in all, quite a handsome looking fellow, the only imperfection being two prominant front teeth slightly protruding like squirrel's teeth, and he has agreeable and winning ways.

December 28, 1880

Garrett and party are met by a mob at the Las Vegas train depot. They want Rudabaugh.

Billy put the same question to everyone who came near him – "This is a terrible place to put a fellow in. Is the jail in Santa Fe any better than this?"

Before Billy returns to his cell he exclaims, "They say, a fool for luck and a poor man for children – Garrett takes them all in."

TRAIN INTERVIEW

As Garrett and his officers stand off the mob, Billy casually talks to a reporter for the Las Vegas Gazette.

"We saw him again at the depot when the crowd presented a really warlike appearance. Standing by the car, out of one of the windows of which he was leaning, he talked freely with us of the whole affair.

"I don't blame you for writing of me as you have. You had to believe other stories; but then I don't know as any one would believe anything good of me anyway." he said. "I wasn't the leader of any gang – I was for Billy all the time. About that Portales business, I owned the rancho with Charlie Bowdre. I took it up and was holding it because I wanted to keep it for a station. But I found that there were certain men who wouldn't let me live in the country and so I was going to leave. We had all our grub in the house when they took us in, and we were going to a place about six miles away in the morning to cook it and then 'light' out. I haven't stolen any stock. I made my living by gambling but that was the only way I could live. They wouldn't let me settle down; if they had I wouldn't be here today." and he held up his right arm on which was the bracelet.

The prospects of a fight exhilarated him, and he bitterly bemeaned being chained. "If I only had my Winchester, I'd lick the whole crowd" was his confident comment on the strength of the attacking party. He sighed and sighed again for a chance to take a hand in the fight and the burden of his desire was to be set free to fight on the side of his captors as soon as he should smell powder.

As the train rolled out, he lifted his hat and invited us to call and see him in Santa Fe, calling out, "Adios."

A MOTLEY CREW

"There is a thin line between catching an outlaw and becoming one."

December 27, 1881

The mob wants "Dirty" Dave Rudabaugh. He killed jailer Lino Valdez last April while trying unsuccessfully to rescue a crony, J. J. Webb. Garrett made a promise to Dave at Stinking Springs that he would take Rudabaugh through to Santa Fe. The standoff lasts for half an hour, before an associate of Garrett's runs up to the engine and opens the throttle. The huge steam engine spins in its tracks for several seconds before rocketing past the platform and leaving the angry mob behind.

It is Billy's first ride on a train. He is as excited as a kid can be.

The possemen have been on the trail for weeks, sleeping in the same clothes, riding in the bitter cold. They look every bit as rough as the men they have captured. To the other passengers, there is no discernable difference between captive and captor.

Due to heavy snowfall, the train stalls at Glorieta Pass for several hours. Billy amuses the boys by ordering a piece of apple pie and placing the entire slice in his mouth. He opens his mouth and – ta da – it's still in one piece.

While Garrett and the possemen yuck it up over this hilarious entertainment, one thing is obvious to the conductor – these boys need to get out more.

Garrett deposits his prisoners with Sheriff Sherman in Santa Fe. There is a small snafu when Garrett orders food for the prisoners and the jailer eats it all.

Above, Billy complains about his treatment from the sheriff. "He lets every stranger that comes to see me through curiosity in to see me, but he will not let a single one of my friends in, not even an attorney. I guess they mean to send me up without giving me any show, but they will have a nice time doing it." Left, Billy begins bombarding the governor with notes like this one.

"In Santa Fe we were allowed to visit the Kid in jail, taking him cigarette papers, tobacco, chewing gum, candy, pies, and nuts. He was very fond of sweets and asked us to bring him all we could."

—MIGUEL I. OTERO

Governor Lew Wallace sketched this drawing of the Palace of the Governors, Santa Fe, New Mexico, 1881

NOTES

March 31, 1880

Wabash, Indiana becomes the first town completely illuminated by electrical lighting.

January 1, 1881

Billy the Kid scrawls a short note to Lew Wallace, "I would like to see you for a few moments if you can spare the time." Wallace is not in his office at the Palace of the Governors, but is on a train speeding towards Washington D.C. to present his new novel to the President.

February, 1881

Sheriff Romulo Martinez plants an informer in the jail and, virtually on the eve of success, Deputy Tony Neis barges into the cell and uncovers a freedom hole. Bonney, Wilson and Rudabaugh hid the dirt and stones in their beds. The bad boys are heavily ironed and guarded around the clock.

March 2, 1881

Billy writes the first of two more

TRAIN PROGRESS MAP

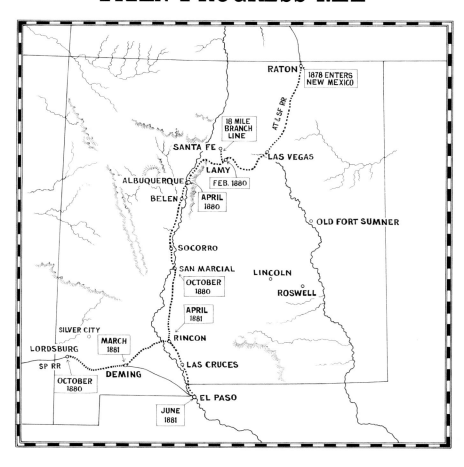

notes to Wallace, who is back from his book tour. This time the Kid tries a different approach – blackmail: "I wish you would come down to the jail to see me. It will be to your interest to come and see me. I have some letters

Judge Warren Bristol

which date back two years and there are Parties who are very anxious to get them but I shall not dispose of them until I see you. That is if you come immediately." Wallace ignores all three notes.

March 27, 1881

The Kid writes his final note to Wallace. "For the last time I ask, will you keep your promise. I start below tomorrow. Send answer by bearer." Billy is referring to his "deal" with Wallace about testifying against the killers of Chapman. Lew is unimpressed.

March 28, 1881

The Kid and Wilson are escorted to Mesilla by deputies Tony Neis and Robert Olinger via the new railroad. At Rincon, an angry mob tries to take the Kid but the deputies back them down. In Las Cruces another crowd gathers, this one more curious than angry. Everyone in New Mexico wants to see the Bandit Boy, but nobody knows what he looks like. As the party, which included the Kid's attorney Ira Leonard, waits on the

The two Deputy U. S. Marshals who escorted Billy the Kid from Santa Fe to Mesilla for trial, Tony Neis (left) and Robert Olinger, March 1, 1881. A local newspaper said Olinger was so big he "had to sit down to keep his head in range of the camera." Note Olinger's gun and knife lying at his feet.

"Advise persons never to engage in killing. "
– BILLY THE KID

platform for the transfer to Mesilla, someone in the crowd says, Which one of you is Billy the Kid?" Billy smiles and puts his hand over the attorney's head and says, "This is the man."

March 30, 1881

Judge Bristol convenes the U. S. district court on the plaza in Old Mesilla. The trial is held in the same room that the Gadsen Purchase was signed. The Kid pleads not guilty to killing an indian agent at the Mescalaro Apache reservation.

April 6, 1881

Judge Bristol dismisses the case and has Bonney rearrested for the killing of Sheriff William Brady.

April 13, 1881

5:15 p.m. – The all hispanic jury finds the defendant guilty and they "assess his punishment at death." Judge Bristol directs that the prisoner be turned over to the sheriff of Lincoln County until May 13 and that on that day, between the hours of nine and three, "the said William Bonney, alias Kid, alias William Antrim be hanged by the neck until his body be dead."

April 21, 1881

Billy is handed over to Sheriff Pat Garrett. Later that day, the two former friends pose in front of the new Lincoln County jail (right), which is the former Murphy/Dolan store. The House will be Billy's final home.

April 28, 1881

Pat Garrett is in White Oaks collecting taxes. Billy asks one of his guards, J. W. Bell, to take him to the outhouse. What exactly happened next will never be known.

'HELLO, BOB.'

April 28, 1881

Bob Olinger is feeding the prisoners at the Wortley Hotel across the street from the courthouse when he hears a shot. He crosses the street and enters the gate to the left of the building. Entering the yard he hears someone call his name from the upstairs window. He doesn't have a chance to answer.

J. W. Bell was shot by Billy while he was running down the staircase inside the courthouse. How and why has been debated for over 100 years. Either the Kid received a pistol hidden in the outhouse, or Billy hit him over the head with his handcuffs and took Bell's gun.

Take your pick.

Billy took an hour to leave and in all that time, not one citizen of Lincoln attempted to molest him.

DREAMS OF SHEEP

July, 1881

Everyone in the territory of New Mexico thinks that Billy the Kid has gone south. Mexico being the only logical destination.

Is it love that draws him north? Or is it the fear of the unknown?

He has danced in the dark with fate many times in his short life, but, as a gambler, he must have known that the cards were bound to turn.

"In the darkness, Death crouched, waiting, ready..."

"When Billy got away from the jail at Lincoln he came from one sheep camp to another up to Fort Sumner."

—DELUVINA MAXWELL

BYE BYE, BILLY

Midnight, July 14, 1881

Three men slip silently onto Pete Maxwell's south porch.

Pat Garrett posts his two deputies at the front gate and goes inside.

Deputy John Poe sits on the edge of the steps in the open gate and Kip McKinney squats just outside. Both immediately notice a lone figure approaching on the inside of the fence.

He is hatless and in his stocking feet. In the moonlight, Poe notices he is buttoning his trousers.

Neither Poe nor McKinney recognize him. Both are from Texas and new to the area. Poe assumes the approaching figure to be a Mexican employee of Maxwell's. Meanwhile, Garrett has awakened Pete Maxwell and is asking the whereabouts of the Kid.

As the Kid mounts the porch he sees the two deputies for the first time.

Alarmed, he brandishes a butcher knife and a self-cocking .41-caliber Colt Thunderer. Springing around like a cat, he demands in Spanish, "Quien es?" ("Who is it?")

Poe rises and tries to calm the agitated stranger.

"Quien es?" demands the dark figure again.

Muerte.

Receiving no reply, he backs into Maxwell's room and directs his question to Pete. "Quien es, Pete?"

Garrett, engulfed in the corner darkness, freezes. He has recognized the Kid's voice immediately.

"He came directly towards me," Garrett recounted. "Came close to me."

Garrett said he dared not speak because his own gun was in its holster, and he was sitting on it!

"He came close to me, leaned both hands on the bed, his right hand almost touching my knee."

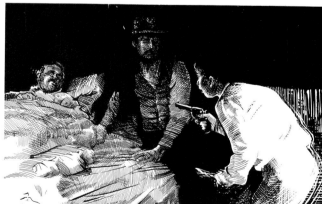

"The Kid must have seen, or felt, the presence of a third person at the head of the bed. He raised his pistol, a self-cocker, withing a foot of my breast."

The Kid jumped back, but instead of firing, he demanded in Spanish one more time, "Quien es?"

Big mistake. Garrett drew his revolver and fired twice.

"The Kid fell dead. He never spoke. A struggle or two, a little strangling sound as he gasped for breath, and the Kid was with his many victims."

UNARMED AND POTENT?

Four men stood over the body of Billy the Kid; Pat Garrett, Pete Maxwell, John Poe, and Kip McKinney.

Garrett had some explaining to do. Billy and he were once friends. So Garrett wrote a book justifying his actions. Ironically, it sold poorly.

Poe agreed with Garrett and said so in print.

Maxwell never talked publicly about the incident.

McKinney, however, confided in a mining partner named Frederick William Grey. Kip told Grey that Garrett learned the Kid would visit his "Mexican sweetheart." The lawmen arrived at the Maxwell house before the Kid and "tied and gagged the girl." Garrett hid behind the sofa and when Billy showed clearly in the open door, Garrett shot him down like a dog.

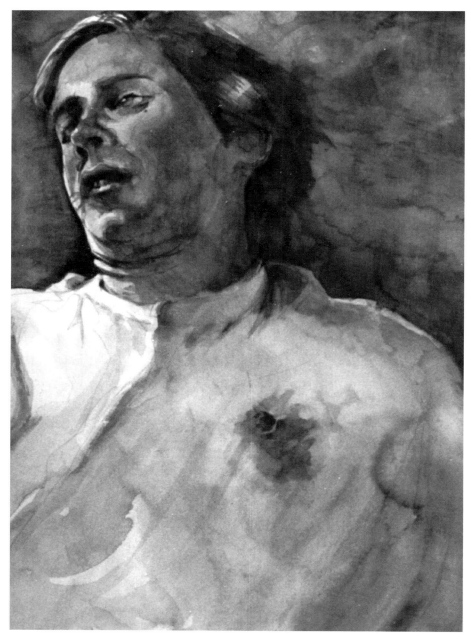

"I think it hard I should be the only one to suffer the extreme penalties of the law."

—BILLY THE KID

KNOCKING ON HELL'S DOOR

July 15, 1881

"'We asked permission to remove the body,' Jesus Silva said. 'Pete Maxwell suggesting removal to the old carpenter shop. We laid the body on the carpenter's bench and placed lighted candles around the corpse. News of the killing spread quickly through the town and surrounding country. And consequently a large number of Billy's friends were gathered at the wake. Everyone's grief at the Kid's death was genuine and sincere. Pat Garrett and his two companions were badly frightened, and did not dare to sleep that night. They remained awake, arms in readiness for any emergency.

"'The morning after the killing, I measured Billy's body and made a rough box we used as a coffin. That afternoon, we dug his grave and buried him.'"

The mourners had to restrain Deluvina Maxwell from attacking Garrett physically. "You piss-pot!" she screamed, "You sonofabitch!"

Years later, Deluvina would say with glee, "I hated those men and I'm glad I have lived long enough to see them all dead and buried."

BEYOND BILLY

As the months roll into years and the century mark nears, the memory of Billy the Kid begins to melt like the adobe walls that once held him.

In fact, the forgetting of Billy, starts early. In 1881, mere months after his death, New Mexico holds a state fair in Albuquerque. In the official program is a running history of New Mexico starting in the 1500s and covering up to the present (1881). There is not one mention of Billy *or* the Lincoln County War. By contrast, Victorio, the Apache warrior, is listed over a dozen times.

The anglo citizens of New Mexico simply wanted to forget Billy the Kid. He was, and to many he still is, an embarrassment. This may explain why Pat Garrett's book on Billy (right), published in 1882, was such a bust.

But the Native New Mexicans never forgot him. He belongs to them – he is one of them. Billy the Kid – the outlaw saint. *San Billito Bandido! Viva El Chivato!*

Long live the Infant Rascal!

"This ruined old wall is tragedy. The past beats against it like a shadowy surge. It stands in monumental vigil over the dead years. Back of it are ghosts. The wind in the cottonwoods above it is like a threnody. It is like a poignant song burdened with the sadness of memories. Gone are the days."

– WALTER NOBLE BURNS

"John Chisum died [of cancer] at Eureka Springs, Missouri, in 1884, and lies buried at Paris, Texas, his boyhood home, and the town he founded is his monument. History has dealt with him meagerly."

—WALTER NOBLE BURNS

GONE BUT NOT FORGOTTEN

Ugly, fat, or fast on the draw, one by one, Billy's compadres join him in the beyond. And thanks to the Kid, we remember them still.

Fred Waite gave up his wild ways, went back to the Indian territory (Oklahoma) and became a respected civic leader. He died one day after his forty-second birthday, September 24, 1895.

"Doc" Scurlock moved to Texas, taught school in Vernon, and refused to discuss his past. He died in Eastland, Texas, on July 25, 1929.

"Dirty" Dave Rudabaugh escaped hanging by tunneling out of the Las Vegas jail. On February 18, 1886, Dave was decapitated by an angry mob in Parral, Old Mexico. His severed head was paraded around the plaza on a pole.

John Middleton opened a grocery store in Sun City, Kansas. The venture was unsuccessful and he came back to working cattle in New Mexico. He died of smallpox on November 19, 1882.

John Kinney served three years in Leavenworth, and then moved to Prescott, Arizona to live with a daughter. He died there on August 25, 1919. His obituary is a joke.

Tom Pickett ended up as town marshall of McNary, Arizona in 1930. He "patrolled the town with a lantern, a big walking stick and a huge dog on a chain."

Henry Brown became Marshal of Caldwell, Kansas. At night, he would moonlight as a bank robber. There was a slight conflict of interest in this arrangement and local townspeople shot him in 1884, when he tried to flee.

Jose Chavez Y Chavez served time in the Santa Fe pen, helped thwart a riot and was pardoned. He died peaceably at Anton Chico.

705 MAIN ST., FORT WORTH, TEX.

Swartz

Above, Jimmy Dolan and his wife Maria Whitlock Dolan taken in 1897, a year before his death.

Dolan had this home built across from the Tunstall store in 1888. It was the showcase of Lincoln. Jimmy can be seen second from right in front of the pillar.

This photo taken in 1990 shows the dramatic change in vegetation on the surrounding hills. One possible explanation is that firewood collection depleted the hillsides.

WINNER TAKES ALL

Even though he will be cast as the villain in countless stories and movies about Billy the Kid, Jimmy Dolan came out of the Lincoln County War smelling like a rose – an Irish Rose.

He never spent a second in jail, even though he was responsible for at least as many murders as the Kid. But more significantly, Dolan ended up with Tunstall's store *and* his ranch!

A respected stockman and Lincoln County leader, he was asked by the Governor in 1895 to write a report on the conditions in Lincoln county for the Secretary of the Interior. In it he has the audacity to write:

"There is but little if any rowdyism in Lincoln County. Our people respect the law and obey its mandates."

In truth there is not a county in New Mexico freer from internal disturbances than in Lincoln.

Susan McSween Barber, aged 74, 1917. Right up to the end she was still objecting to "being made out a middle-aged woman, when she was much younger," in the movie *Billy the Kid* starring Johnny Mack Brown.

Lincoln, September 16, 1991. Casa de Patrón, the building at left, is today a successful bed and breakfast. The town has changed little in the last century. Compare this scene with the picture on page 51.

Cattle and sheep have greatly advanced in value, grass was never finer than now and crops have never given fairer returns. The result is that our people are prosperous and happy, content with their lot, and realizing that the sun never shone on a fairer section of country than ours."

He was county treasurer for two terms and a member of the territorial senate. He died at the ranch on February 26, 1898 of a "hemorrhage of stomach." Frank Coe said it was delirium tremens.

NEW MEXICO'S CATTLE QUEEN

Susan McSween never understood the fascination with Billy the Kid and "those foolhardy boys" who had gotten her husband killed. She remarried on June 20, 1880 to George B. Barber. A gift of cattle from John Chisum started her on the road to becoming a highly successful stock raiser. She became known as the "Cattle Queen of New Mexico." She divorced George Barber on October 16, 1891 on the grounds that he had abandoned her. She was feisty to the end and she breathed her last in the sparsely furnished bedroom of her little house at White Oaks on the evening of January 3, 1931.

GARRETT GETS HIS

Pat F. Garrett
Collector of Customs
1903

Pat Garrett rides Billy's coattails all the way to the White House. Over the objections of his staff, President Teddy Roosevelt invites the famous sheriff to Washington, D.C. in early December 1901, and nominates Pat to be Collector of Customs at El Paso.

Supposedly, there was concern that the former sheriff could not read. The President handed Pat this note and asked him to read it aloud and sign:

"I, the undersigned, Patrick F. Garrett, hereby give my word of honor, that if I am appointed Collector of Customs at El Paso, Texas, I will totally abstain from the use of intoxicating liquors during my term of office."

Garrett smiled, signed the note, and said, "Mr. Roosevelt, it suits me exactly."

By repeating the words aloud,

The photos that lost Pat Garrett his commission.

Pat can be seen in the above photo taken at the 1905 Rough Riders convention in San Antonio, Texas. He is at the table of honor, fourth from the right, across from the President. The bottom photo, however, is the one that got him in trouble. Pat introduced his friend, Tom Powers (in high crown hat, third from right), as a "cattleman." Garrett lied because if Teddy knew the truth – that Powers was actually a saloon owner and gambling buddy of Garrett's – it would reflect badly on Garrett. As it turned out, when the photos were leaked to the press, the President "growled furiously" about being made a chump.

Garrett was not reappointed. Ironically, Powers remained friendly with Roosevelt and later brought the President a pet bear cub which he nick-named "Teddy" – as in "Teddy Bear."

PAT GARRETT WHO KILLED 'BILLY THE KID' DIES IN ROW

Albuquerque, N. M., Feb. 29.—Pat Garrett, the man who killed "Billy the Kid" in a desperate gun fight a number of years ago and who has a reputation all over the West for his ability to shoot straight, was shot and killed today at Las Cruces in a gun fight.

Garrett was a personal friend of the president and once held the position of internal revenue collector at El Paso. He was the most famous character of the frontier left in New Mexico, having been a soldier, scout, Indian fighter and all-around gun man.

At six-foot four, with hat and high-heeled boots, Pat Garrett stood almost seven feet. It is easy to see why Billy described him as "one long-legged sonofabitch."

Garrett proved he could read; by signing the statement, he proved he could write. And, by doing both, he took an oath not to drink.

This is the high point of his career. Garrett immediately grates on everyone in his new position. He ends up in a fist fight with a former employee. His administration is tainted with accusations of "gross neglect and suspicious dealings." When his term is up, he is not reappointed (see left).

Garrett returns to his delapidated ranch, 25 miles east of Las Cruces. He speculates in mining, he tries to practice law in Old Mexico, but mostly he drinks and is disagreeable. His enemies hate him and his friends do not understand him. He is quarrelsome and insulting.

The end comes on February 29, 1908. While riding in a buckboard, Garrett encounters a 21 year-old cowboy named Wayne Brazel who is running goats on Pat's land. While stopping to urinate, a bullet slammed into the back of his head.

Brazel was arrested but aquitted, claiming self-defense. This prompted Garrett's biographer, Leon Metz to dryly comment, "The only time in history a man has been assassinated while urinating that the defendent claimed self-defense."

The Denver Post, February 29, 1908

"Escupe en el cielo y regresara"

—OLD VAQUERO SAYING

KIP MCKINNEY

1906

The only known photo (above) of the man who was with Garrett when the Kid was brought down. He is the lanky one in the rocker. His full name was Thomas Christopher "Kip" McKinney. This photo was provided by his grand-daughter, Mrs. Carl Ruby Faubion to the Lincoln County Historical Society. The family says that Kip was six feet six inches tall and a lawman in his own right. Some two months before Bonney was killed, Kip shot and killed Bob Edwards, described as "a notorious horse thief from southwest Texas." Edwards shot Kip in the neck, but the bullet missed the jugular. Garrett and McKinney tried hog farming for a time. The family resents the inference made on page 100. Hilton Wayne McKinney, son of Kip's son, says, "Irresponsible writers [like the one who wrote this book] are the reason my grandmother and grandfather did not cooperate. My grandfather was a professional. Poe, Garrett, and the others were not. They needed the glory to hide their insecurities."

"They needed the glory." Left to right, Pat Garrett, James Brent and John Poe (who was also with Garrett on July 14, 1881). All three were Sheriff of Lincoln County at one time. Brent's advice on gunfighting was simple and to the point:" Get your pistol out and cocked, making haste slowly."

THE RESURRECTION

1925

He is forgotten.

One man brings Billy the Kid back from the dead. He is Walter Noble Burns, a sports writer from Chicago. He comes out to New Mexico in 1924 and interviews the old-timers who are still kicking– The Coes, Susan McSween, Sally Chisum, Paulita Maxwell Jaramillo. He even interviews people who are dead– like Pat Garrett– which casts suspicion on his veracity.

Burns claims he wrote for "tired businessmen."

His book, "The Saga of Billy the Kid" is published in 1925 and holds several distinctions: it's the first Book of the Month Club offering, and it's the first book on Billy that treats him as the good-bad boy. The book is an immediate best-seller and not only does it revive the Kid, but it spawns countless books and articles and movies, until Billy the Kid passes Jesse James as America's most written about and filmed outlaw (Jesse has had 11 movies made about him, the Kid —42 and counting).

As Burns' work is examined more closely by historians and Billy Buffs, the mistakes mount up. Example: Burns said that O'Folliard was killed on Christmas eve—it actually occurred on December 19.

By the fifties, Burn's book is viewed as "pure fiction," and worse– "a fantasy."

It's more than a little ironic that most of Burns' harshest critics were attracted to the legend of Billy the Kid by reading "Saga."

BURNS MAKES HIS CASE

Highlights from the censored chapter:

For the one woman of his dreams, he risked his life in desperate chances. For love of her he died...Paulita Maxwell, clothed with romance in the tradition of the Southwest as the heroine of Billy the Kid's one genuine love affair, is Mrs. Paulita Jaramillo of new Fort Sumner today.

...The name of Mrs. Paulita Jaramillo recurs time after time with the effect of a motif as you follow the trail of Billy the Kid today through the country his exploits made famous...

...[A neighbor of Paulita's claims] there is no secret about it. Billy the Kid was madly in love with Paulita. After his escape from the gallows at Lincoln, he came straight to Fort Sumner to see her, though it seemed the road to sure death. They planned to elope to old Mexico and be married...

...Frank Coe at his ranch on the Ruidosa warms to the mention of Mrs. Jaramillo's name. " beautiful girl," he says. "I knew her well and must drop her a line for old time's sake. She was the only woman Billy the Kid ever sincerely loved except his mother."

Matin Chaves of Santa Fe says: "I talked with the Kid as he passed through Las Tablas after his escape at Lincoln. I advised him to leave the country and seek safety in Mexico. 'Not yet,' he answered. 'I am going to Fort Sumner to see the girl who is to be my wife. If I die, all right; then I will die for her.'"

James H. East, afterwards marshal of Douglas, Arizona, was with Pat Garrett in the fight at Tivan Arroya in which the Kid was captured. When the posse passed through Fort Sumner with the Kid as a prisoner, East and Lee Hall, acting as his guards, took the Kid with Garrett's permission, to the Maxwell home to say goodbye to Paulita.

"We took the Kid," said East, "into a room in which were Paulita, Mrs. Luz Maxwell, her mother, and Deluvina Maxwell, an old Navajo family servant. Mrs. Maxwell wanted us to let Billy and the girl go into the next room for a last word alone together. But we suspected that was a ruse to give the Kid a chance to escape and we would not permit it. The meeting between the Kid and his sweetheart was affecting. He held her in his arms as she wept on his shoulder. When it came time to take the trail for Vegas, we almost had to tear them apart, much to my regret, for all the world loves a lover."

John W. Poe, banker of Roswell, who was with Garrett when the Kid was killed, said shortly before his death in 1923; "Paulita Maxwell was awakened by the shot that killed her sweetheart. It was generally reported that she and the Kid were to be married and I was rather surprised that she showed little emotion when she stood beside his dead body."

The chapter killed by attorneys.

"... I will say that I would not have hesitated to marry him and follow him through danger, poverty, or hardship to the ends of the earth in spite of anything he had ever done or what the world might have been pleased to think of me. That is the way of Spanish girls when they are in love."

– PAULITA MAXWELL

WAS SHE, OR WASN'T SHE?

Walter Noble Burns was convinced that Paulita Maxwell was Billy the Kid's true love and that it was for her he died.

She, of course denied it and insisted that Billy was in love with another Fort Sumner girl – Celsa Gutierrez.

In a letter to a friend, dated June 3, 1926, Burns lays out his case:

"In this first version I came out flat-footedly and said Paulita Maxwell was the Kid's sweetheart and it was to see her that he went to Fort Sumner after his escape from Lincoln and was killed. But my publishers thought this chapter too frank and believed that it might lay them open to a possible suit for libel. So I rewrote this chapter to make it safe. Mrs. Jaramillo denied to me that she was the Kid's sweetheart and I had to print her denial but as you may have noticed I told all about the old stories of her romance with the Kid. But I had to let her deny them. That was the only way out of it. I thought it almost ruined the story of this very interesting and romantic episode but my publishers insisted."

John Henry Tunstall, 1873

GEN. LEW WALLACE'S

BEN-HUR

Illustration by Bob Steinhilber

NIGHTMARES OF SHEEP

For all his scheming and planning, John Henry Tunstall sleeps a troubled sleep.

Had he merely stayed in Santa Barbara and bought land at the inflated price of 20 dollars an acre, there might be a street named for him today. As it is, he ventured to a place where land prices are still depressed a century later. His family in England lost their suit against the U.S. government and never received a penny.

His exact grave site is unknown.

THE GOLD MINE BIBLE STORY

Lew Wallace's New Mexico mining investments never really paid off, but his paper scratching certainly did. *Ben Hur*, the novel Wallace sweated over in the governor's palace, became an international sensation. Published in November 1880, sales increased at a steady rate until, by 1885, sales averaged seventy-five copies a day.

In the next several years it would sell over a million copies and eventually appeared in twenty-one languages. Then came the Ben Hur toys, Ben Hur cigar, bicycle, baking powder, perfume, tobacco and even candy. Not to mention the movies.

Lew looked at his wife and said, "My God, did I set all of this in motion?" They both cried all the way to you-know-where.

WHAT IF?

Do we remember him because he died so young? What if Billy had survived? Would his story resonate into the present?

June 15,1931

PORTALES, N.M.—John Henry Bonney, of this city, figures his father deserves a place in the annals of Wild West History. Mr. Bonney, 45, has written a manuscript detailing the exciting life of young "Billy" Bonney who, according to the author, had many hair-raising tales as a lad which heretofor have never been told outside of the immediate family.

John Bonney relates that his father, who passed away last July, took part in a "war" that occurred near Ruidoso. "Billy" Bonney was sometimes known as a "Kid," and he supposedly once jumped out of a burning house because of an insurance policy. He was eventually pardoned for his crimes and married Paulita Maxwell, of Old Fort Sumner, on December 20,1885. The newlyweds bought a ranch near Crow Flats in the Guadalupes and started a family.

The Bonney family is well-known in the Portales area. William Bonney, Sr., had been a successful stock raiser here for several decades and his son and grandsons carry on the tradition. William Bonney's other son, "Billy," Jr. died in WWI.

"I would like to take this opportunity to exonerate his memory a little," John says, "and relieve myself of the feeling that by not telling this important story, I am letting my father down."

He calls his manuscript, "The Authentic Life of a New Mexico Cow-Boy." So far, no publisher has agreed to print the story of this interesting pioneer, but John Bonney remains hopeful.

The William H. Bonney Family, taken at Weed, New Mexico, 1888. Left to right: William H. Bonney, Jr., age 3; William Sr., 28; Paulita Bonney, 27; John Henry Bonney, 2.

THE DAWN OF A NEW LIGHT

July 16, 1945

He has seen it all. Francisco Gomez rode with Billy the Kid and on Susan McSween. He survived them both. Now he is alone and all the others are gone.

Late one July night in 1945 he is a witness to the light coming up over the mountains from Alamogordo. It floods his adobe ranch house and arcs across the Capitans. As the light recedes he feels the past slip deeper into the darkness. His memory spans from the Spanish ox-cart to the Trinity Site of the Manhattan Project.

From Billy to Atomic bombs– not a bad stretch for one lifetime!

BILLY ON THE BRAIN

Real Billy

First attempt, July 1958.

After taking art at the University of Arizona, 1965.

After flunking out of art school, 1969.

He is as elusive on paper as he was in the flesh. Here are 21 attempts at his likeness – one for every year of his life.

Retard Billy

Rudolph the red-nosed Billy

Manson Billy

Billy l'orange

Boy Billy

"The Boss" Billy

Stonehenge Billy

Beatle Billy

Goofy Billy

Chubby Billy

Alfred E. Billy

Brushy Billy

Degas Billy

Ball-point Billy

Madonna Billy

Saint Billy

Saint Billy2

Jesus Christ! Enough Billies already!

Billy the Kid, Starring Robert Taylor, MGM, 1941.

He never robbed a bank or a train. He never appeared on a wanted poster. And he never stood in the street and dared another man to "draw."

MOVIE MYTHS

He killed 21 men–one for every year of his life.
It sounds so poetic, but alas, his actual tally is closer to four.

He carved notches on his gun for every man he killed.
Jim East, one of the men who captured Billy at Stinking Springs says, "I never saw a six-shooter with notches filed upon it, except to sell to a tenderfoot. A man that kills people doesn't want to advertise it."

The Kid killed his first man at age 12 when a bully insulted his mother.
Absolute hogwash.

Billy the Kid was quick on the draw.
He may have been faster than greased lightning, but the Kid never stood in the street face to face with another gunfighter to shoot it out–but then almost nobody else in the Old West did either. Thank you, Hollywood.

THE 66 KID

Little Boze Billy

August 1958

An Arizona family, returning from a vacation in Thompson, Iowa, pulls into a dusty parking lot just off of route 66 near Santa Rosa, New Mexico.

A young kid with big ears piles out of his parents 1957 Ford and scrambles inside.

He had spotted the Old West Museum on the family's way to Iowa and his Norweigan father has begrudgingly allowed him to pick *one* stop on the way back.

The excited kid tries to take in the rambling array of wild west artifacts in a single swoop.

Finally, he makes his choice, pulls out a quarter his grandfather gave him and buys an "authentic" photo of Billy the Kid.

Twenty-eight years later, he discovers the photo is a fake and makes a vow to someday put out an entire book full of fake photos.

"What people choose to believe – is a fact in itself."
- LEON METZ

"Billy the Kid just keeps riding across the dreamscape of our minds – silhouetted against a starlit Western sky, handsome, laughing, deadly. Shrewd as the coyote. Free as the hawk. The outlaw of our dreams – forever free, forever young, forever riding."

NEW MEXICO MAGAZINE
PAUL ANDREW HUTTON,
JUNE 1990

**Right: "San Billito Bandido"–
Saint Billy Bandit**

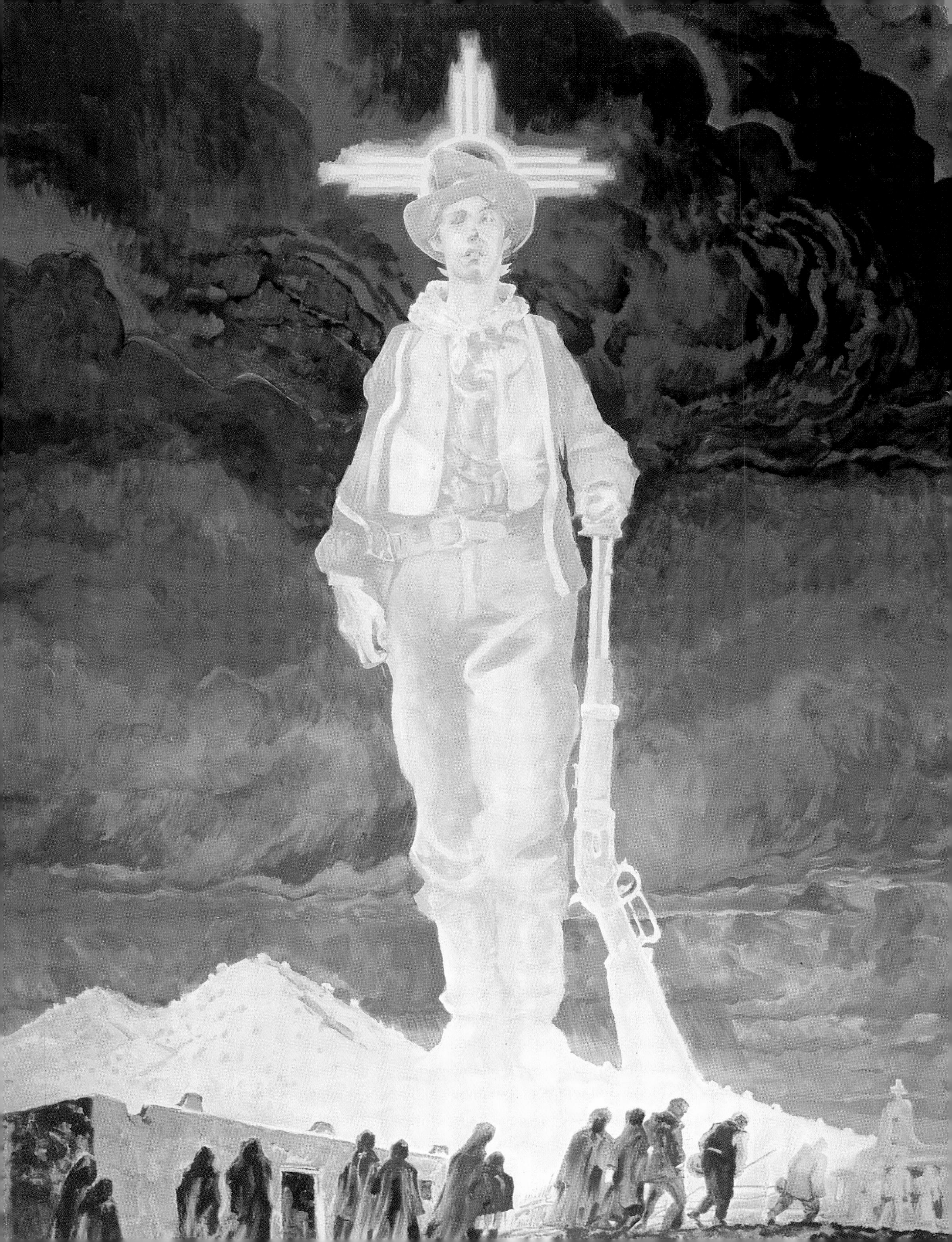

CREDITS

*This book is dedicated
to my parents;
Bobbi Guess Cady, who lit the fire,
and my father, Allen P. Bell,
who kept throwing on the fuel.*

DESIGN AND COMPUTER GRAPHICS
Julie Sigwart

Photo Research, Jerry Weddle; **Maps and Cover Lettering,** Bob Steinhilber; **Cover Design,** Dan Harshberger; **Photography,** Ed Mell, Ralph Rippe; **Computer Graphics,** Dave Ritter

MODELS
Billy, William H. Cox, John T. Holbrook, Tony Tullis, Jeremiah Douglas
The Arizona Rangers, Thunderbolt, Richard Dobberstein, Gary Lehmann,
Jim Fowler, Barb Kemp, David Dixon, Ruth Dixon
Pioneer, Arizona, Big Ed Douglas, Jenny Smith
The MTM Ranch, Charles Motley, Todd Masden, Jackie Masden, Alexander Curtis,
Steve "Handy" Rinsem, Flint Carney, Dakota Giago, Thomas Bell, Alex Whitehurst,
Mathew Whitehurst, Deena Bell, Tamara Peterson
Arizona Territorial Shooters, Philip Carlin, Dan Jewell, Ross Seymour
Grand Canyon Railway, Tom Kelley

CONTRIBUTORS, CATALYSTS & INVALUABLE CONTACTS
To Kathy, who hates Billy the Kid but loves me,
John Gilchriese, Bob McCubbin, Jerry Weddle, Fred Nolan,
John Sinclair, Nora Henn, Walter Henn, Sadie Pearl Duncan, Charlie Waters
Taplou Weir, Jerry Scott, Kim Scott, Jerry Jordan, Cleis Jordan,
Billy the Kid Gang, Joe Bowlin, Maryln Bowlin, Paul Northrop, Jayme Northrop,
Billy Brainerd, Bob Hart, Chuck Parsons, James Dunham,
Otilia Flores, Mike Pitel, Janean Grissom, Don Lavash, Herb Marsh Jr.,
James Ballinger, Jim Earle, **Old West Outfitters**, Jeff Gordon, Jeanne Sedello, Sylvia McNeil,
Paul Taylor, Randy Sawyer, Danny Delgado, Jose Israel Castellanos, Dick George,
Gregg Clancy, Suzanne Brown, Linda Corderman, Gary Bennett, Bob Earley, Lee Scott Theisan, David K. Jones, Dave
Walker, Fanchon Edgar, John Giese, Steve Randolf, **Recursos** Marcia Byrom Hartwell,
Chris Sicurella, Theresa Broniarczyk, **Tri Star Commercial Printing**

REAL PHOTO CREDITS
There are many real photos in this book and I would like to thank the following individuals and organizations for allowing me to use their wonderful photos: Bob McCubbin for the use of his extensive collection, including the photos on pages 15, 22, 34, 45, 93, 103, 104, 111. Jerry Weddle for the use of his excellent collection, including the photos on pages 25,27, 28, 63. Frederick Nolan for the photo on page 18. Irene Kennedy for the photos on pages 25, 28. Paul Northop for the photo on page 105. The University of Texas at El Paso for the photos on page 106. The Haley History Center for the photos on pages 10, 14, 107. The Lincoln County Heritage Trust for the photos on pages 14, 70. The University of Arizona Special Collections for pages 11, 16. The Chaves County Historical Society for the photo on page 108. The Museum of New Mexico for the photos on pages 15, 30. The Silver City Museum for the photo on page 12. The Collection Centre Canadien d'Architecture/Canadian Centre for Architecture, Montreal for the San Francisco panorama on pages 18 and 19. University of California at Berkeley, 88; Brigham Young University, 91.

"Spit in the sky and it comes back."
– OLD VAQUERO SAYING